Household Feng-shui

Household Feng-shui

By Living Buddha Lian-sheng Sheng-yen Lu

Translated by
Janny Chow

Purple Lotus Society
San Bruno, California, U.S.A.

Household Feng-shui
First Edition
Copyright © 2002 by Purple Lotus Society,
San Bruno, California

Library of Congress Cataloging-in-Publication Data

Lu, Sheng-yen, 1945-
    [Yang zhai di ling chan wei. English]
    Household Feng-shui / by Living Buddha Lian-sheng;
    translated by Janny Chow.
        p.cm.
    ISBN 1-881493-09-1
    1. Feng shui. 2. Geomancy. I.Chow, Janny, 1952- II.Title.

BF1779.F4 L82513 2002
133.3'337--dc21
                                        2001048516

Printed in the United States of America, 2002

About the Author

● Living Buddha Lian-sheng is a prominent religious figure throughout Southeast Asia. As of 2002, over 5 million people have taken refuge in his True Buddha School. With over 300 chapters worldwide, the True Buddha School is recognized as a major component in Buddhism today.

● Living Buddha Lian-sheng was born in 1945 in Taiwan. In 1982, he settled in the United States to promote Buddhist teachings in the West. He has since built a major Buddhist temple, the Ling Shen Ching Tze Temple, in Redmond, Washington, and a large retreat center in the Cascade Mountains.

● Originally a Christian, Living Buddha Lian-sheng was twenty-six years old when a profound mystical experience led him to study Taoism, Sutrayana, and Tantric Buddhism. After intense training and practice over a period of fourteen years, he became a Master of exceptional accomplishment in these disciplines and achieved Perfect Enlightenment.

● By practicing the True Buddha Tantric Dharma, as taught by Living Buddha Lian-sheng, one can realize Awakening and Liberation in this present life.

● Living Buddha Lian-sheng is also a prolific writer, having published over 152 books in Chinese on such varied topics as Tantric Buddhism, Geomancy, Zen Buddhism, and Taoism. Many of these books are now being translated into English.

Acknowledgments

The translator would like to thank the following persons for making this book possible:

Living Buddha Lian-sheng Sheng-yen Lu for His blessing and guidance; Master Lian-hsiang for her encouragement; Master Samantha Chou for her encouragement and support; Master Lian-chi (Chiu Hung-kang), Ven. Lian-mou, and Ven. Lotus Duck-wah for their feng-shui workshops which were invaluable in clarifying the meaning of the many feng-shui terms; Ven. Lian-kai (K.C. Ng) for proof-reading, Pamela Ziv Johnson for editing; Christine Chan for editing and desktop publishing; and Cheng Yew Chung for the cover design.

Table of Contents

PART II

Preface—An Offering of Feng-shui Knowledge to my Readers

This is a book of "worldly Dharmas." It is a book of methods used to secure success in the mundane world—it's goals being family harmony, good health, wealth, successful careers, filial obedience from one's children, and the mitigation and eradication of disasters.

In past feng-shui readings, I noticed that many people live in homes shockingly unfavorable to them. My sympathy and compassion for those living in such unlucky houses prompted me to write this detailed geomancy book *Household Feng-shui*. So that this book can be read and understood by everyone, I have used the clearest possible language to explain the deep and profound study of "earth magic."

I, Living Buddha Lian-sheng, feel there are three fundamental aspects to any successful "worldly Dharma" or mundane endeavor:

1) timing — the karmic opportunity bestowed by the Cosmos or destiny

2) the support of people — man-made factors such as self effort and harmonious human interaction

3) a favorable geographic position — assistance rendered

1

in the form of a positive environment, or favorable feng-shui

"Time, people, and place" are the three constituents behind any successful endeavor in the mundane world. The factor of "time" is usually very difficult to change. The second factor, "people," generally involves the exertion of great effort on one's part. The final factor, "place," is the easiest to manipulate. Thus, geomancy (feng-shui) becomes an effective method of bringing about radical change or reversing the course of events in a particular situation.

"Place" also plays a role in the cultivation of "transcendental Dharma," or spiritual transformation. In the olden days, Taoist practitioners sought famous mountains and caverns, places of exceptionally high energy, to cultivate. Today, practitioners of esoteric Buddhism still seek out caves of high energy to conduct their retreats.

In my younger years, as a student of the Taoist Master Ch'ing Chen, I was imparted the teachings contained in the manuscript *The Secrets of Earth Magic*. To a certain degree, my knowledge of feng-shui has aided in the founding of the True Buddha School and my attainment of Enlightenment through Buddhist cultivation. Whenever I relocate, I always select a locale with the best feng-shui. My careful attention to the role played by feng-shui has enabled me to keep my spiritual energy at a perpetually full and vigorous level.

In all my life, I have rarely fallen ill. I do not take afternoon naps, and I never feel tired. I have lived in the United States for five years now and have never even had the common cold. This is a result of the opportune combinations of "time, people, and place." In fact, my transformation into "Living Buddha Lian-sheng" is concrete proof of the ideal integration of these three factors of "time, people, and place."

For a Taoist practitioner to succeed in cultivation, he or she must have certain innate qualities, be hard working and perseverant, and have assistance from "earth energy." Therefore, the selection of an "ideal place" to cultivate is very important. In ancient times, all great Tantrayana adepts found caves with strong earth energy to cultivate. Without the contributing energy from such locations, their great efforts would have been in vain.

In view of the above principle, homes with positive earth energy will not only bring its inhabitants a sense of well-being, but good health, successful careers, and family harmony as well. Conversely, the inhabitants of homes lacking positive earth energy experience adversities, emotional dissatisfactions, and failing careers. With one event feeding the next, such inhabitants may become trapped in a vicious cycle of disasters.

Many students and readers have requested that I write a feng-shui book on homes. After careful consideration, I also feel a need for more people to understand the important role of "earth energy" in our lives. Humans should have access to the great knowledge of feng-shui and develop a proper view of the benefits of earth energy.

Inherent in the art and science of feng-shui are many guiding principles for life. I will make every effort to write in a manner that is clear and easy to understand, incorporating practical concepts and examples. It is my wish that, through a detailed description of my own experiences, some of the biases and incorrect views about feng-shui will be rectified.

In this book, I shall discuss the important aspects pertaining to the selection of a home—the location, altitude, width, door, surrounding environment, living room, kitchen, bedroom, shrine, bathroom, office, and staircase positioning—and discuss different feng-shui theories.

I hope the writing of this book will offer an impartial and systematic view of feng-shui that will be of practical value to its readers. This resource book reveals that my teachings do not lean toward total renunciation of worldly affairs but are an amalgamation of both "transcendental" and "worldly" Dharmas. The publication of this book is an offering of boundless blessings to all my students and readers. It is my wish that everyone will attain good health and longevity, auspiciousness, a harmonious family life, an increase in wisdom and fortune, and fruition in spiritual cultivation.

Sheng-yen Lu
True Buddha Tantric Quarter
17102 NE 40th Ct.
Redmond, WA 98052
USA

March 1987

PART I

1. Avoid Living in a "High Peak" Spot

One time a rich man invited me to do a feng-shui reading for his luxurious home. At the appointed time, he showed up at my residence in an expensive sedan. However, I did not have any intention of leaving with him.

"It is about time. Shall we leave now?" he asked.

"I am sorry, but I don't think I need to see your house," I replied.

"Why?" He was taken aback by my response.

"I already went to see your home last night. I understand the whole situation now."

"Master, you did what?" His lower jaw dropped in amazement.

Such an event was not a new experience for me. The previous night, during my sleep, I had exited my body through the crown chakra. After ascending to the sky, I had flown speedily through the clouds and arrived at his house. The home of this rich man was built at the highest point of an eight-acre lot that encompassed the peak of a tall mountain. Surrounding the huge house itself was a wall made of iron railings.

I told him, "You have two horses, one brown and one white.

Inside your house, there are six fireplaces. They were all lit when I visited last night. You have two very valuable and famous paintings in your collection. I also saw an antique sword from a long time ago…"

The rich man was astounded. Finally I told him of the undesirability of living in a "high peak" spot. A high spot opens one to the blowing of winds from all "eight directions," resulting in "feng-sha" (noxious wind energy). To be in a "peak" spot is to stand out exposed, without any protection or support.

Among the rich, there are some who, because of their wealth, feel they are above others and want to live at the highest spot in town. They purchase land at peak sites and build luxury homes. After houses of this type are erected, however, their owners' fortunes often quickly plummet. Because land at the highest point is exposed to the assault of winds from all directions, the chi, or life-giving energy, at such homes is most unstable. Ten out of ten such homes turn into unlucky abodes.

At high peak sites, the "earth chi" is usually non-circuitous and unable to accumulate, and is, therefore, weak, loose, and dispersed. Building a home on such a site will definitely cause a decline in one's fortune. Only under one condition is a "high peak" site a good choice for building a home—when the earth chi travels in an upward and spiral path. If this is the case, earth dug up at the site will display a five-colored, variegated spiral pattern. However, such an earth chi pattern is extremely rare among tall peaks. One can virtually rule out "high peak" sites as ideal areas to build homes.

As written in *The Secrets of Earth Magic:*
The highest spot definitely invites assault and attack.
The peak spot definitely invites isolation.
The chi of a home built at the highest point disperses quickly because it is subjected to the blowing of winds from all direc-

tions. Also, such a home, by being so conspicuous, often falls prey to burglars and thieves. An analogy can be made to a person who rises to a high position and attracts too much attention. People then become jealous of him and want to get rid of him. The President of the United States, for example, because of his position as commander-in-chief, requires the protection of security personnel at all times.

Peak spots do not have any higher geographical features in the vicinity to support them; therefore, the earth chi at such abodes disperses quickly and does not accumulate. People living in such abodes will become incompatible with one another and develop unsociable and eccentric dispositions. It is inevitable that inhabitants of peak houses will suffer the break-up of their families and wind up alone.

The same principle also can be applied to houses built on level ground. If one feels that one is head and shoulders above everyone else, and deliberately builds a house higher than those surrounding it, one is also inviting assault and isolation. An exception to this would be if the inhabitants have already accumulated enough merits and status to match such a house.

If a person is without merits and status, it would be extremely inauspicious for him to live in a house that is taller than all surrounding houses. This will incur disasters and great failures. It is my opinion that there should be a correlation between the status of a house and the status of its inhabitants. Ignoring the form of the house or failing to make a status match may lead to unfortunate events beyond one's imagination.

Therefore, my advice is that, unless one is of high merit or status, it is inauspicious to live in a house that stands conspicuously taller than the surrounding houses. It is also inauspicious to live in a house that stands in isolation, apart from other surrounding houses. These houses fall into the "high peak form" category.

The rich man who had invited me to do a feng-shui reading for his home eventually sold his luxurious peak villa because he knew that the previous owner of the house had failed in his business and that one of his servants had been murdered. Indeed, at the time he had come to see me, this rich man had just divorced his wife and separated from his children. It was a pattern that fit the consequences of "assault and isolation." Therefore, one must pay careful attention to the selection of a building site.

2. Avoid Living in
"Low and Overshadowed" Areas

In my younger days, I performed numerous feng-shui consultations. The one rule I always maintained was to treat everyone equally, whether they were rich or poor. When the rich came to seek my services, I gladly advised them. When poor families approached me for help, I gladly accepted their invitations.

During these times, whenever I agreed to feng-shui readings, I also stuck to one important principle: I never asked for a service fee but allowed the other parties to pay whatever they wished.

Since my only motive for studying geomancy was to help people, I have done readings for very poor families. One such family, whose head of the household made a living selling vegetables, lived in a very low area at the foot of a broken precipice that rose in a steep wall to the sky. The area around the house was surrounded by bamboo. After studying the house and its surrounding geographical features, I came to the conclusion that the house fit the pattern of that of a "low and overshadowed" house.

As written in *The Secrets of Earth Magic:*

The lowest site will meet suicide.

The overshadowed site will encounter unexpected hardships.

My analysis turned out to be an accurate one. After a fight caused by their declining financial situation, the owner's wife committed suicide by drinking insecticide. The grandmother of the household became half paralyzed from a severe case of rheumatoid arthritis. One child was afflicted with polio, another with asthma. The owner himself, who worked as hard as he could to sell his vegetables, was facing a crushing defeat.

Why are houses built in low and hollow sites tied to the fate of suicide? This is because such houses are always in an inferior position. People living in such houses develop emotional blockages and have trouble seeing their own ideals fulfilled. Due to their frustrated emotional state, they often fail to find safe exits when angered or provoked. Also, low and hollow sites are sites of "yin" energy, where disembodied spirits and ghosts like to converge. "Yin spirits" may play mischievous tricks on one and engender thoughts of suicide.

The close proximity of the tall and broken cliff to the house created a feeling of being "pressured and overshadowed." This "suppression" type pattern predisposes one to strange illnesses. The closeness of the tall and broken cliff also provoked a sense of desolation and misery. Living in such a house, one would never have the opportunity to become wealthy.

There is also a more realistic problem for homes built in the hollows at the foot of mountains. During rains, water accumulates and does not drain quickly. When earthquakes strike, an avalanche may bury the entire house. How can one not be wary of the inherent problems of such sites?

I asked the owner of the house, "Are there seven inhabitants in your house now?"

He gave me a puzzled look. "There are only five."

I smiled and said, "There are indeed seven, although two of the seven could be considered frequent visitors."

He replied, "We rarely have any visitors."

I asked him to check with the grandmother to find out if there were, indeed, two visitors at their house. To his surprise, the grandmother confirmed my words. She described seeing a man in black and a woman in red, in Ch'ing Dynasty attire, frequently entering and exiting their home. This reply brought great shock to the owner.

"Why didn't you tell me earlier?" he asked the grandmother.

The grandmother replied, "I was worried you might be frightened. Besides, I didn't think you would believe me. You would probably have accused me of hallucinating and becoming senile."

I told the owner that the low and overshadowed site was unsuitable as a residence because it encouraged the convergence of yin spirits. A healthy person living there would become ill and encounter numerous hardships. Oftentimes, due to the influence of disembodied spirits, one may succumb to their calling and attempt to commit suicide.

The grandmother was aware of the yin spirits because she was at the end of her years. The yang energy in her body was dispersing as yin energy accumulated, and this had led to an opening of her psychic vision.

Some feng-shui practitioners believe a low and hollow site accumulates chi from the water element. Because water is regarded as the equivalent of money, such a site is considered a wealthy spot. However, ensuring optimal movement of "water chi" into such a site requires proper handling by a skillful feng-shui master. This involves creating a proper inflow of "major water chi" and an outflow of "minor water chi." Otherwise, the sole inflow of major water chi without an outlet, will cause every resident of the home to become "engulfed by the water."

A house built upon a site that is too low and too hollow is therefore inauspicious. It is also inauspicious to have a tall, broken cliff directly behind (or to either side of) the house as this overshadows the house.

I remember, after the reading, receiving a red envelop with fifty Taiwanese dollars (approximately U.S. $1.25 then) from the owner. I did not mind the amount because I knew they were poor, and I was not a feng-shui master who sought to profit from his consultations. Feng-shui, as a worldly Dharma, is merely a skillful means. More important is the goal to move and inspire people to practice the "transcendental" Buddhadharma.

So, before selecting a building site, one should first inspect the terrain. This is just too important a factor to ignore. Too high a terrain invites "feng-sha" (noxious wind energy); too low a terrain invites "shui-sha" (noxious water energy). An ideal site is neither too high nor too low.

The study of the feng-shui of homes is actually a study of balance and harmony. To learn feng-shui, one must first master "the art of balance and harmony."

3. Avoid Living in a Site Affected by Noxious Spirits

I once performed a feng-shui reading for a very quiet, elegant home. Located in a nice neighborhood, the house had a fine shape and an auspicious floor plan. The furniture had even been arranged to conform to the rules of feng-shui. The owner of the house had previously consulted several famous feng-shui masters and had been told that everything was fine. However, as soon as I stepped inside the house, I could sense something unusual about it.

"I don't think there is anything wrong with the feng-shui of this house, but there is something strange in the air, a presence of unusual spirit energy," I told the owner.

The owner asked me, "In which particular spot of the house is this energy the strongest?"

Tuning into my extrasensory perception, I walked through each room of the house until I came to the swimming pool located in the backyard. Stopping before it, I said, "This is the spot."

The owner remarked, "Living Buddha Lian-sheng, you are indeed extraordinary. Many unusual happenings have occurred right at this swimming pool."

The owner then recounted the following occurrences: People swimming in the pool experienced intolerable coldness after staying in the pool for a short while. Every person who swam in the pool developed leg cramps. A person swimming alone would occasionally feel tugs at his legs, and if he swam underwater, he would feel the presence of another person swimming alongside him. Sometimes, late at night, when there was no one swimming, the sounds of water play could be heard.

"Oh! There are noxious spirits dwelling here," I said.

After looking into the matter, it was discovered that before the construction of the current house, an old hospital had stood on the site. The current swimming pool was where the morgue of the hospital had been. Due to the hospital's old age and other requirements for the land, the hospital had been torn down and replaced. However, the spirit energy of the original hospital had not dissipated, and this led to the manifestation of strange phenomena.

A house can inherit "noxious spirits" from the earth upon which it is built because such spirits have previously existed within the earth. Examples of such sites are ruins of temples, hospitals, cemeteries, old battlefields, execution grounds, murder scenes, disaster scenes caused by fires, earthquakes, or other calamities, and shrines. If, for no reason at all, strange phenomena and mishaps occur at such sites, it is usually due to the presence of "noxious spirits." Homicides also occur unexpectedly where noxious spirits are present.

To deal with such situations, some feng-shui masters advocate the bulldozing and removal of fifty centimeters of topsoil from the original site and replacement of the old soil with clean soil. Removing earth possessed by spirits is one way to control noxious energy.

However, if a home has already been built upon the site, one can only use one of the following "averting" methods:

Taoist practitioners may use the "Nine Phoenix Pure Water Method that Removes Impurities." (This method was discussed in one of my previous books.)

Buddhist practitioners may first chant the Great Compassion Dharani, to prepare the Great Compassion Dharani water, then sprinkled this water from the inside of the house to the outside. One should then prepare sections of green bamboo, shave off the skin, and write on each section the Earth God Mantra of "Om, du-lu, du-lu, di-wei, so-ha." One must then stick these bamboo sections into the earth surrounding the house, as a means to restrain the ominous energy. This signifies that spirits attached to the soil cannot disturb people living on that piece of land, nor can they enter into the land anymore.

More conventional methods include the sprinkling of holy water by Catholic priests, the Taoist purification method, and the Buddhist rituals of compassionate chanting and Bardo Deliverance.

Not all homes afflicted with noxious spirits were built on land once occupied by temples, cemeteries, hospitals, battlefields, or execution grounds. I had once done a reading for a home with noxious spirits whose owner was a connoisseur of antiques. He had amassed a collection of antique beds, tables, shrine tables, and utensils, some of which had "spirits" attached to them. His whole family had been thrown into turmoil without knowing the cause.

Also, certain areas attract noxious spirits simply because the earth chi is strongly "yin" to begin with. Spirits and ghosts love to assemble at such places; these include dark cinemas, deep and secluded valleys, unusual castles, and old houses.

Most feng-shui masters do not have cures for a home whose energy has been arrested by spirits. My study of the spiritual world has given me insight into the "noxious spirits" that cause energy disturbances. Feng-shui is the art of balancing the magnetic, subtle energy field of a house or building. If the energy of the house's magnetic field flows smoothly, it's inhabitants feel peace and comfort. If this magnetic field is disturbed, chaos arises, and people living in the house experience agitation and roadblocks in their relationships.

Noxious spirits are invisible. According to *The Secrets of Earth Magic*, the presence of noxious spirits means the house is haunted. For ordinary people, it is better to avoid living in such haunted houses. However, I, Living Buddha Lian-sheng, love to live in haunted places because I can convert the disruptive vibrations of these entities into harmonious frequencies. By befriending the ghosts, they become one's helpers. Feng-shui professionals need not fear noxious spirits as they can be recruited to increase business, harmony, and success in one's life.

4. Avoid Living on Odd Shaped Lots

What are odd shaped lots? Odd shaped lots are incomplete or fractional lots. In terms of the five elements:
— Round shaped lots are associated with metal.
— Rectangular lots are associated with wood.
— Broom or irregularly shaped lots are associated with water.
— Triangular lots are associated with fire.
— Square lots are associated with earth.

In urban areas, most odd shaped lots are triangular or irregularly shaped, and neither is suitable for residence.

It is difficult to design floor plans for triangular shaped houses, and the disorderly and asymmetrical pattern of irregularly shaped houses also poses problems to the design of a harmonious floor plan. In selecting lots, one should avoid odd shaped lots, even though they may be cheaper. These lots invite noxious chi, and people living in them are gradually subjected to noxious influences and may develop "fragmentation." A comparison may be made between the shape of a house and that of a human being. An incomplete lot is analogous to a person with missing or deformed limbs and facial

19

features.

A triangular lot with one of its apexes positioned in the front invites "huo-sha" [noxious fire energy], and its two sides, the left and the right, invite "feng-sha" [noxious wind energy.] An irregularly shaped house, due to the presence of too many angles, invites harm to oneself or others. Therefore, in purchasing a lot to build a home, one should look for a square, rectangle, or circle and stay away from odd shaped lots. An odd shaped lot may be considered for the construction of commercial buildings, as long as no one lives there.

A common element shared by most odd shaped lots is the presence of one or more protruding features. Protruding features are associated with extremely strong energy forces, and inhabitants who live for a long time in such houses come under these influences and become extreme in their personalities. The magnetic or subtle energy field of such sites is "strong and chaotic" and may also increase the risk of accidents for the inhabitants.

People living in houses with strong magnetic forces do not experience peacefulness. If it is a commercial building, such as a bank, hospital, supermarket, or department store, (where there is a great deal of foot traffic), then a strong magnetic force might actually be beneficial. An expert feng-shui master would know the method to divert the excessively strong energy in an auspicious direction and thus bring more business to the merchants.

On the other hand, if the excessively strong magnetic force of an odd shaped lot is not directed in an auspicious direction, the strong force will attract scoundrels with ill intentions resulting in bank robberies, medical disputes, burglaries, and frauds, which are most abhorred by businesses. A "dynamic force of vitality" indicates auspiciousness. In contrast, the occurrence of crimes such as arson, murder, rape, and lascivious behaviors at such properties is an indication of the presence of noxious energy.

If the strong subtle energy can be guided in an auspicious direction, it will result in a "dynamic vitality." If it is led, instead, in an inauspicious direction, it will result in horrible crimes. An expert feng-shui master would be someone with the knowledge to direct the earth chi.

I performed a feng-shui reading for a family whose house was built on an odd shaped lot. When I met them, the family was extremely down on its luck. The inhabitants had already been involved in five different car accidents, some of which were quite serious. Also, every member of the household displayed some kind of neurotic behavior. I noted that these harmful effects were caused by the triangular shaped house in which they lived.

The family members had hot tempers and were easily provoked to anger. The owner and his wife quarreled daily, and their children were involved in gang activities. Such extreme behavior develops over time from the influence of noxious fire energy from the apex at the front and noxious wind energy from the two sides of the triangle. The house was built upon a triangular lot formed by intersecting roads.

I noticed that the bedrooms were all pointed in the front and wide at the rear, due to the constraints of the house shape. I told the owner, "Your daughters will become men's mistresses."

"Master Lian-sheng, your psychic reading is extremely correct."

"It is not from my psychic reading. When one's bedroom is lopsided, one, of course, cannot become a legal wife but only someone's mistress," I responded. The owner's two daughters, who were quite beautiful, had both fallen in love with married men. Besides their involvement with gang members, they seemed especially attracted to married men.

"What is there to do?" The owner was quite sad.

"Do not continue to live on an odd shaped lot. It is better to move. Find a nice, quiet house somewhere else and convert this house into a shop. This would benefit both you and the house."

I, Living Buddha Lian-sheng, believe it is best to stay away from odd shaped lots because they possess both the characteristics of "fluidity" and "extremeness" which embody violence and chaos. Whenever such lots are used for commercial buildings, an expert feng-shui master should be consulted to ensure the proper guiding of the "chaotic chi" in an auspicious direction. If the "chaotic chi" is not carefully handled, it may bring violence instead of harmony. Such noxious disharmony can be extremely fierce. Just the thought of such upheavals is enough to make one shudder.

5. Keys to the Selection of Home Sites

A part from the "high peaked," "low and over-shadowed," "haunted by noxious spirits," and "odd shaped" sites mentioned in the previous chapters, there are many other places that are inauspicious and thus unsuitable for building homes. In selecting a site, it is essential that one consult an expert feng-shui master and invite him or her to give the place a thorough reading.

In places where the soil is predominantly sandy, the building of homes is not advised. Earth chi dissipates quickly in sand, and therefore such places lack an abundance of earth chi.

One may also rule out rocky ground because earth chi also dissipates quickly there. Sites with an absence of "nurturing chi" can cause more harm than good.

Soil with good earth chi is part clay and part ordinary soil. There should be enough cohesiveness in the soil for it to form a clump when held and clenched in a fist.

It is also best if the rear of the lot is slightly more elevated than the front. Such a geographical feature indicates the presence of a "back support" as well as having a "proper receptacle" for receiving the converging earth chi. Houses on such sites are sitting properly on "chairs" provided by the great earth.

Before constructing the house, one should inspect the right and left sides of the site for any geographical "armrests." "Armrests" represent "guards" as well as "benefactors," and they also symbolize the "storing and accumulation of chi," indicating that help will come in many forms.

A desirable front view from the house consists of a wide vista that is flat or sloping slightly forward, as long as there are no broken cliffs or deep hollows. It is even better if the vista includes a scenic lake in the distance. Having other houses situated directly across from one's house is fine as long as one's front door does not directly face the corner of any house.

Actually, the four major rules for selecting a tomb site may also be applied to the selection of a residence. These are: "having back support," "having armrests on the left and right sides," "having a 'reflective' body of water in the front," and "having an island in the water." These four principles for selecting a "yin abode" [for the deceased] are the same as those for selecting a "yang abode" [for the living].

Building sites in cities are generally quite flat, but by observing the direction of the flow of rivers or other watercourses, one may determine which spot is more elevated and which is lower. Pay attention to the cohesiveness of the soil. Scan buildings on both sides to see if they are neat and pleasing to the eye. Take into consideration the possibility of any front view obstructions occurring after the house is completed. As one generally plans to live for a long time in a custom built home on a selected site, a beautiful view day-in and day-out helps soothe one's mind.

On the other hand, if the front view is a garbage dump, an electrical pole, the corner of somebody's house, or a chicken farm, it may create obstructions and unpleasantness in the atmosphere and cause roadblocks in the emotional well-being of the whole family. The earth chi may also be destroyed if one grows vegetables or other crops in front of the house, digs a manure pit in front, and uses chicken manure stored in the pit to fertilize the plants. One should be wary of and pay particular attention to these other features, which also have great bearing on the earth chi: a garbage incinerator in front of the home, an approaching road that runs into the front of the house, a chimney in front of the house, and temples in front or behind the house.

Before purchasing a site, one needs to find out about the history of the land. Paddy fields, dry farmlands, woods, farms, factories, pastures, roads, and grasslands are auspicious. Sites after fire disasters, hundred-year-old houses, execution grounds, cemeteries, temples, hospitals, crematoriums, isolated tomb sites, and historical monuments are inauspicious for building homes.

If one wants to build a home on land where there has been a chicken farm, livestock ranch, or pig farm, one must first dig up fifty centimeters of the top soil and replace it with clean earth. Once this is done, the land will be all right.

If one must build a home on land occupied by noxious spirits, one should avert future obstacles by first making peace with the spirits and having the land cleansed. Buddhist monks or nuns may be invited to chant sutras to help deliver the spirits and pray for peacefulness.

When I, Living Buddha Lian-sheng, do feng-shui readings for residences, I always first inspect the land before the house itself. This is to study the overall earth energy. If the overall energy is vigorous, people living there will definitely prosper. If the overall energy is weak, the luck of the occupants will definitely go downhill. Big houses should be paired with strong earth chi, while small houses must be paired with earth chi that matches the smaller size.

Building a small house on land with great earth energy is a waste. Building a grand home on land with weak earth energy invites decline.

Another factor to consider is that, in urban areas, roads radiate in all directions. Cars speeding on the roads also contribute to the overall atmosphere of the environment. Some roads are straight while others zigzag and are winding.

Straight roads can cause the problem of "an oncoming charge of chi directed at one." Winding roads can create "an outside the bow situation" specific to curves.

It is best to avoid building homes on sites that are charged by oncoming roads or on the convex side or outside of a curve. I shall explain these factors in detail in a later chapter. (A site facing an oncoming road may be used for the building of a police station, civic hall, or temple.)

I am aware that, to this day, some people still regard fengshui as mere superstition. The truth is, feng-shui is not superstition, but rather the study of the environment at a profound level. A beautiful environment naturally leads to beautifying of the mind and spirit. When one's mind and spirit are in peace and harmony, one will succeed in one's endeavors. After all, when Mencius [a sage and student of Confucius] was a child, his mother relocated their household three times, just so she could find a perfect and beautiful environment to raise him in.

What this chapter consists of are of course only the most basic principles in selecting a home site. There are many detailed and more profound principles that I will go into in the future, as the opportunities arise. It is my hope that this book will provide a clear introduction of feng-shui to its readers.

6. Nature Thrives in the Essence of Love and Perishes in its Absence

The most famous verse written by Master Hung-jen, the Fifth Zen Patriarch, is as follows:

Seeds sowed with the essence of love,
Grow to bear fruits;
In the absence of the essence of love or seeds,
Neither nature nor life exists.

This verse is also most appropriate when applied to the art of household feng-shui. According to *The Secrets of Earth Magic,* the decisive factor determining the prosperity or failure of a house is the "essence of love" or the absence of it.

With the essence of love or affection — the household thrives.

Without the essence of love or affection — the household declines.

This quality, this "essence of love," can be detected in a house just as it can be detected in a flower. When a flower blooms lusciously, exuding a wonderful fragrance, it is in its most beautiful and glorious moment. When a flower is wilted and lifeless, its petals brittle and dry, we know instinctively that it has come to its moment of decline.

In the study of human faces, a vital and healthy complexion with expressive eyes full of sensitivity indicates the "essence of love." On the other hand, a face that is expressionless, listless, grayish or pale with little vitality is a face indicative of the absence of the "essence of love." The idiom "a widow's face" has been used conventionally to describe someone completely devoid of youthful vigor and passion.

In analyzing residences, it is a great art to distinguish ones with the "essence of love" from ones that do not have this essence. When the exterior of a house appears lively and dynamic, without any clashing elements, it can be described simply as having the "essence of love." Many houses with multiple protruding angles also may look very dynamic, but if clashing features exist everywhere, then they lack the "essence of love."

Houses that are too overbearing, greatly flawed, unpleasantly plain, or look ridiculous and unreasonable belong to the category of houses that "lack the essence of love."

A true feng-shui practitioner can observe a house's exterior and quickly determine whether or not it has the "essence of love." This knowledge is gained only after many years of keen observation and practice. Upon seeing a house, an experienced feng-shui master can assess with certainty whether the "essence of love" exists.

I, Living Buddha Lian-sheng, feel that the judging process is one that depends entirely on one's senses and cannot be conveyed through words. It is a skill that requires years of field training to develop. Experienced masters know what to look for, while inexperienced ones will not be able to put their finger on it. A truly capable feng-shui master can, with a "sniff" of the house, know if the "essence of love" exists or not by observing its chi.

This is the secret key to the studying of a house's exterior.

In addition, a house's "essence of love" also depends on the "magnetic birth orientation" of its owner. Every individual is born with two major "lucky" and two major "unlucky" orientations within the 360 directional points of the compass.

When the orientation of a house is compatible with the magnetic birth orientation of the owner [i.e., if the orientation of the house correlates to an orientation that is favorable to the owner], then the "essence of love" exists in that house.

When the orientation of a house is not compatible with the magnetic birth orientation of the owner, then the house lacks the "essence of love."

Therefore feng-shui professionals generally base their judgment of a house on how favorable its orientation is in relationship to the owner. If the orientation of a house is compatible with the owner, then it will bring great fortune and prosperity. If there are clashes or incompatible situations, then misfortune and disaster will follow. This is entirely based on the theories and principles of "magnetic birth orientation."

In general, feng-shui masters use the system of twelve directional points in which the twelve Earthly Branches are matched with twelve of the specific directional points of a compass. Every person is born under one of the twelve Earthly Branches, each of which has an animal symbol attached to it. The twelve Earthly Branches are: tzu, ch'ou, yin, mao, ch'en, ssu, wu, wei, shen, yu, hsu, and hai. However, some feng-shui masters also prefer to use the system of twenty-four directional points. Still others prefer to use the Nine Stars or Eight Directions methods. My personal feeling is that the twelve directional points method is most correct, although a combination of various methods may also be used.

Therefore, in my opinion, the two basic elements used to determine the luck of a house are its "orientation" and "external appearance." If the orientation of a house is favorable to the owner of the house, then the next thing to consider is its exterior. Before building a house, one might consider consulting a true feng-shui expert because the exterior appearance of a house often determines whether there will be the presence or absence of the "essence of love," peacefulness or misfortune, and auspiciousness or disasters.

I was once invited to do a feng-shui reading for a western-style villa. After walking once around the house, I spoke with certainty to the owner, "Whoever lives in this house has tumors in the body."

The owner asked in astonishment, "Master, how do you know?"

"How can I not know! There are tumors all throughout this house."

Later I found out that the mistress of the house had had tumors in her uterus, intestine (three of them), and the stomach as well. She has had numerous surgical operations!

The exterior appearance of a house plays a very important role. If it is dynamic, with smooth architectural lines that do not clash with the environment, then it has the "essence of love" and will definitely bring prosperity to its inhabitants. Otherwise, it will bring forth decline.

"*Nature thrives in the essence of love and perishes in its absence*" is indeed a golden saying.

7. Correlations between a House and the Human Body

According to my guru Taoist Master Ch'ing Chen: "After living in the same house and having been subjected to the same environment and magnetic field for many years, a person gradually takes on the characteristics of his house."

In *The Secrets of Earth Magic,* the following comparisons are made between a house and the human body:

The front of a house is analogous to a person's facial features. The left and right sides are like the upper and lower limbs. The living room is analogous to the heart. The bathroom is like the kidneys. The kitchen is analogous to the liver. The bedroom is like the lungs. The dining room is analogous to the spleen.

Based on the above analogies, defects in certain areas of a house can imperceptibly influence the health and fortunes of the head of the household. Of course, correlation between specific parts of a house and those of a human body cannot be one hundred percent accurate. Just as some people use the living room for dining purposes and others have a bathroom installed inside their bedroom, there is sometimes not a clear-cut division between the various functions of the rooms.

Yet, Taoist Master Ch'ing Chen told me that a feng-shui expert can indeed, after careful assessment of the house, determine its problems.

In the past, when I performed feng-shui readings for others, I often pointed out to my students structural features which constitute risks for "surgeries" and "abnormal growths." Shortcomings found in houses which present "surgical risks" are: incomplete enclosures around the house, a skylight in the roof, unbalanced windows in relation to the house, casual positioning of doors, too many doors leading to the outside, or inappropriate and unbalanced positioning of doors inside the house. All these are characteristics of "surgical cases."

Which structures pose risks for "abnormal growths," such as tumors or cancers? During the surveying of the house, pay attention to any "protruding features" which clash with the rest of the house. Look for things that do not match the house and look as if they were attached or added on (like a person carrying a backpack). The mismatch may be in size or in symmetry. One has to pay attention if such "protruding features" exist because they constitute a risk for abnormal growths.

I, Living Buddha Lian-sheng, am rather opposed to the idea of reconstructing or adding extensions to an existing building. For example, when there is nothing wrong with the original design of the inside of a house, owners often get the notion to have a certain part of the house pulled out and rebuilt. Or, they suddenly may decide to build a little adjoining house to the back of the big house. Once the little house is added, it completely changes the feng-shui of the entire structure.

One should know that structural renovations inside a house indicate "surgeries," while adding extensions to the outside of a house indicate "extra growths."

Sometimes, structural demolition and rebuilding of houses are done too casually. If the rebuilding and additions are appropriate, they do not matter. However, if new clashes are created, they become risks for surgeries or growths. This is because any demolition or rebuilding causes changes in the feng-shui and magnetic field of the house. If the changes create a better feng-shui and magnetic field, then they are fine. Otherwise, bad changes may be followed by great disasters.

Before initiating any structural renovation or extension, it would be best if one consulted with a feng-shui expert. The selection of an auspicious date from the Chinese almanac for the commencement of construction is very important. Structural renovations or extensions, like surgical operations, can do great harm to the body if botched.

I personally pay careful attention to house repairs. If a window is broken, a pipe is leaking, a wall is cracked, water or electricity is not running, or any household appliance is broken, one should have them repaired as soon as possible. These minor repairs do not cause any change or threat to feng-shui. However, if they remain un-repaired inside the house for a long time, they can affect one's psychological well-being and, consequently, one's fortunes. Therefore, try not to store any broken items in the house. If there are any problems with the water or electrical supply, have them repaired as quickly as possible.

There is an analogy between house repairs and preventive health care. A minor cold, if not taken care of, may worsen and develop into secondary pneumonia or even kidney problems.

I was once visiting with a friend, and I told him curtly, "Everyone in your family will undergo surgeries."

"Why?" asked the host.

"Because a hole has been dug right next to the stomach of

your house."

The owner of the home had wanted a shortcut from the street to his house, so he had had the wall closest to the street demolished, creating a special driveway while keeping the second level of the house intact.

Strangely, in each of the three years following the creation of the new driveway, a family member had undergone surgery. The host asked me if there was any way to resolve the problem without taking out the driveway.

I picked a "Man" [meaning full] date from the Chinese almanac and performed a "repair ritual" to erect an invisible wall. As expected, from then on, no one in the family has required surgery. The "repair ritual" indeed works wonders.

8. Balance is Auspiciousness

Someone once asked me, "Among the many house forms, which kind is best?"

I replied, "Any form that is balanced is auspicious."

At first glance, it might seem that an architecturally balanced form would be a simple concept to detect, but, in reality, it can be quite complicated.

Some people enjoy novel and unusual designs and have built houses in strange looking shapes. As long as these designs comply and do not clash with the principle of the constructive movements of the Five Elements, then these may still be considered balanced designs. For example, in Tantric Buddhism (based on the association between the five chakras and the Five Enlightened Wisdoms) stupas symbolizing the five chakras have been constructed consisting, from top to bottom, of the following shapes: dome, elongated semi-circle, triangle, circle, and square.

The Five Elements are fire, wood, water, metal, and earth. According to the principle of the constructive movements of the Five Elements, earth generates metal, metal generates water, water generates wood, and wood generates fire. Using this principle, one can build structures based on shapes of the Five

Elements, arrange them in a clockwise fashion, and devise novel, unusual, and original designs.

Generally, unless one seeks to be deliberately "stylish," any conventionally balanced house is very auspicious.

One important aspect that needs to be taken into consideration is the balance of the "dragon side" and the "tiger side" of the house. When standing at the front door facing outside, the "dragon side" is to your left and the "tiger side" to your right. The ideal condition is to have the "dragon" and "tiger" balanced.

A tall dragon may be balanced by a long tiger, or a long dragon balanced by a tall tiger. Geomancers generally consider a taller or longer dragon to be auspicious and a taller or longer tiger to be inauspicious.

The most auspicious house shape has a "green dragon" and a "white tiger" matching and in balance.

There is a feng-shui verse that states —

When a sharp peak emerges from White Tiger Hill,
The wife will definitely abuse the husband.

This verse describes a situation in which the white tiger is taller than the green dragon. It also implies that a servant may dominate his master, or that there may be a reversal of roles between the male and female, with the yin overpowering the yang. As a result, the environment may be one of disharmony and imbalanced earth energy that invites the malign force of "sha-chi," portending great misfortunes.

I once performed a feng-shui reading for the abbot of a monastery. The monastery, with its back NNE, faced the SSW direction, with the feng-shui compass indicating the trigram "ken." Water at the front of the monastery flowed from east to south (from the chen position of the Later Heaven Sequence to the ch'ien position of the Former Heaven Sequence, as shown on the compass). There was no prominent topographical armrest on either side of the monastery, and I also noticed that the abbot's living quarters was not located at a commanding position, but rather at a site right below the White Tiger Hill.

I asked the abbot, "Who lives in the White Tiger Hill?"

"The disciples," he replied.

"Soon your post will be taken from you," I said to him.

"Why?"

"The circumstance here is that of a subordinate overtaking the master; it will only be a matter of time before you lose your position."

The abbot was an honest monk, and he was visibly saddened by my feng-shui assessment. Several years later, however, I heard he was no longer the abbot of the monastery.

A taller or longer white tiger signifies the presence of an overpowering force. Most people living in places with a high White Tiger Hill will gradually develop nervousness, power cravings, competitiveness, or start harboring dark schemes against others. In short, there will be no auspiciousness or peace in such a situation.

When buying land to build a house, one must figure out clearly which direction the house will face, as the direction the front door faces plays an extremely critical role. It is best that the direction be favorable to one as determined by one's date of birth. Pay attention to the matching of the green dragon and white tiger. Do not allow the white tiger to be taller or to stand out because this signifies great misfortunes. It will be too late for regrets once disasters occur.

Of course, there are Taoist and Tantric methods to avert and remedy bad feng-shui situations such as this. These methods belong to either the "suppression category" or the "remedy category" and may provide temporary resolutions.

General feng-shui practitioners may be able to assess a situation and offer resolutions, but they may not necessarily understand that implicated in the art and science of feng-shui are the principles of Tai Chi, Two Forms, Four Appearances, Five Elements, Eight Trigrams, and other principles governing the workings of the universe. In a place where there is a clash or assault of noxious chi, one can transform the adverse situation into a peaceful one using the "suppression method." Such remedies, in fact, not only avert disasters, but may result in great benefits as well. Their efficacies are indeed inconceivable.

At places [on the dragon side of buildings] where I, Living Buddha Lian-sheng, have installed stone tablets for the dragon spirit, people have often seen golden and green lights. Some have even seen the green dragon and heard its roaring sounds. Lights bright as the sun and the moon have been observed emanating from the sites. To resolve the problem posed by a white tiger that is too tall, it is necessary to install, on the dragon side, Living Buddha Lian-sheng's green dragon stone tablet.

9. Outside the Bow and Inside the Bow

"Outside the bow" — When we raise a bow and mount an arrow on the string of the bow, the area pointed at by the arrowhead is considered "outside the bow."

"Inside the bow" — When we raise a bow and mount an arrow on the string of the bow, the segment of the arrow located within the bow is considered "inside the bow."

In simple terms, a bow is an arc. The area enclosed by an arc is called "inside the bow." The area outside an arc is called "outside the bow."

For example, we can draw a circle and place a house inside this circle. The house would be "inside the bow," no matter which direction it faces. On the contrary, houses outside the circle are all located in an "outside the bow" position. In terms of topography, watercourses, roads, and buildings can give rise to "outside the bow" situations.

An "outside the bow" situation created by a watercourse occurs when a meandering river flowing in front of one's house forms a curve, and the house is located outside the curve. An "outside the bow" situation created by a road occurs when a meandering road in front of one's house forms a curve, and the house is located outside the curve.

An "outside the bow" situation created by another building is a situation that happens to houses located in the vicinity of large circular shaped stadiums, as they are all located outside a curve.

In household feng-shui, houses enclosed by a topographical or structural curve are located "inside the bow." An "inside the bow" position is one that is being nurtured by "affection" and will see great prosperity.

In contrast, houses located on the outside of a curve created by landforms or other structures are in the path of forces bouncing off the curve. Such "outside the bow" houses lack the essence of "affection" and will see decline.

In general, three phenomena can be created by a landform or building structure: "inside the bow," "outside the bow," and "straight." The latter situation occurs when the watercourse or road that passes in front of one's house is straight, and there is no curved building in front of one's house.

A true feng-shui practitioner will select "inside the bow" sites to build homes and avoid constructing houses in areas that are "outside the bow." This is because "outside the bow" sites are like "targets" being aimed at by arrows and under the assault of malign forces from all directions. In terms of earth energy, such sites are directly confronted by "sha-chi" or noxious chi from all sides. When one is under the invisible ill influences of "sha-chi," one will definitely encounter great disasters or major accidents.

I, Living Buddha Lian-sheng, have noticed that many contemporary luxury homes have been built "outside the bow," facing the direct aim of arrowheads. I could not help but sigh at these luxurious "masterpieces" designed by professional feng-shui consultants. I shudder to think that such feng-shui professionals can be so ignorant and incompetent! I knew of one rich man whose home had been built "outside the bow." Originally a powerful businessman, immediately after moving into his new home, he was seriously injured in a car accident. After the incident, his business also suffered great setbacks and orders for his company took a nosedive. The disastrous "outside the bow" position also caused his employees to embezzle money from him. It was quite a sad state of affairs, and soon after, the large, luxurious mansion became vacant.

I find that many contemporary feng-shui practitioners like to pay particular attention to the direction a house faces. They favor houses with front doors facing southeast, south, or east. Houses facing southwest, northeast, and west are undesirable, while those facing northwest and north are average. Thus many feng-shui practitioners concentrate on juggling the direction faced by the front door.

The correlation between the orientation of a house and the magnetic birth orientation of an individual is of course important, but whether a house is located with its front door facing the outside of a bow or the inside of a bow is even more important.

I would like to stress:

"Inside the bow" = Great Auspiciousness

"Outside the bow" = Great Misfortune

If one has already purchased a site that is "outside the bow" on which to build a home, or if one has already built a home on a site that is "outside the bow," how can this be remedied? A true feng-shui master will offer the following two resolutions:

1) "Copying the same curvature" — For example, a large building located outside a ring can adopt a curved design to its structure. A design conforming to the same curvature as the topographical curve is the best method to prevent the ill influences of an "outside the bow" situation. Adopting the same curvature on the building structure will render the "sha-chi"

ineffective.

2) "Equal retaliation" — For example, design the building in the vicinity of a circle in a curve form that has the same but opposite curvature as the circle. The malign forces directed toward one by the curve of the circle will be rebounded by a similar curve inherent in one's house design. The forces generated by the two "outside the bow" positions will cancel each other out.

I deeply feel that there is an intimate relationship between an "inside the bow" position and the presence of "essence of affection," as well as between an "outside the bow" position and the absence of "essence of affection." This is a relationship that involves the principle of earth energy and its movements. Based on personal experience studying the various elements of topography and landscape, one can judge if a house is auspicious or not. The levels to be considered are very complicated but, when each level is analyzed, one can determine if a house is "within the bow," "outside the bow," or "straight." By carefully studying the phenomenon of "inside the bow," "outside the bow," and "straight," one will discover great and mysterious correlations among "heaven," "earth," and "men."

10. The Positioning of the Front Door

In general, feng-shui practitioners regard the northeast and southwest positions as "ghost door" positions. Doors are therefore never installed at these two positions.

The front door should be installed in an orientation compatible with the birth magnetic orientation of the head of the household. Doors are "chi entrances," and main doors are "major chi entrances." For people living in modern apartment buildings, the main entrance on the ground floor is the "major chi entrance," while the entryway to their apartment is a "minor chi entrance."

Just as a person's mouth can have a great impact on one's life, a house's front door plays a critical role in dictating the lifeline of the house. There is a common Chinese saying that "via the mouth, illnesses find their way in (through unhealthy eating habits) and disasters find their way out (through unwise words)."

Some geomancers hold the following opinions:

— A front door facing east is most appropriate for businesses or commercial properties because east is associated with the rising sun and vitality.

—A front door facing south benefits politicians, religious heads, and industrialists. Historically, Chinese emperors built their palaces overlooking their subjects to the south. Nevertheless, my opinion is that one should avoid positioning the front door facing east or south if one's magnetic birth orientation happens to be incompatible with facing east or facing south.

A student had once asked the question, "Should a front door be positioned in the middle, on the dragon (left) side, or on the tiger (right) side?"

"You have asked a question that hits upon my secret to the positioning of front doors!" I replied.

When Taoist Master Ch'ing Chen taught me *The Secrets of Earth Magic*, he explained that the positioning of the front door should be determined by the flow of "shui-shen" or "water spirit" [watercourse]. This is a great feng-shui secret!

Middle door — A middle front door should be constructed if "water spirit" chi accumulates in front of the house. This would be the case if, for example, the front of the house faced a lake or ocean. Also, when building a house upon flat ground, where the land is without hills or sloping gradients, a middle front door is appropriate.

Dragon door — When "water spirit" flows from the tiger side to the dragon side, a dragon door is appropriate. That is, if, from the inside of the house looking out, land to the right is more elevated than land to the left and the watercourse flows from right to left, the house should have a dragon door.

Tiger door — When "water spirit" flows from the dragon side to the tiger side, when the left side of the land is more elevated than the right and water flows from left to right, the house should have a tiger door.

This simple secret to the positioning of front doors is priceless. A door positioned according to this principle will have an ample supply of "water spirit" chi, the chi that brings money. This chi will flow naturally through the "chi entrance" into the house, filling it with wealth.

I once helped a businessman reposition his company building's front door. Upon such a locale, the building should have had a dragon door but had a tiger door instead. He had reached a nadir in his business ventures, and despite great efforts, was unable to solicit any new orders. Employees were working inefficiently and business had virtually come to a halt. After the rearrangement of his front door, the reception of "water spirit" chi into the building led to the company's complete turnaround. The first business transaction immediately after the repositioning was a success, and everyone's spirits lifted. Business began to flourish and employee confidence greatly improved.

Thus, the prime factor determining whether a middle, dragon, or tiger door should be installed is the directional flow of "water spirit" and the best positioning of the front door to receive this chi.

Another student asked, "What can be done when the front door's position is incompatible with one's magnetic birth orientation?"

"One can re-position the doorframe," I replied.

By re-positioning the doorframe, its orientation also changes. One can even re-orient the frame by a ninety-degree turn. All architects know how to design and re-orient doorframes, and by doing so, the orientation of the whole house is not changed, only the direction faced by the front door.

Another student asked, "What if a house should have a dragon door but has a tiger door instead? A bedroom is located on the dragon side making the creation of a dragon door there practically impossible. What then should be done?"

Taoist Master Ch'ing Chen has taught me the following

remedy for such a situation: a feng-shui practitioner can place a stone tablet (or rock) on a selected spot so that the "water spirit" chi, when flowing from the tiger side to the dragon side, collides with the stone tablet and is rerouted towards the tiger door.

Master Ch'ing Chen used the game of billiards to illustrate this secret method. To send a billiard ball into a pocket, one must utilize the "rebound" force from another ball. When using this feng-shui approach, the "water spirit" chi strikes against the stone tablet which redirects the chi into the house.

Locating the site for the positioning of the stone tablet, however, requires the expertise of a true geomancer. For the stone tablet to be efficacious as an enhancer of benevolent energy, it should also be installed using appropriate Taoist rituals and prayers.

My methodology for deriving an auspicious orientation for a front door is based on the theory that each of the twelve Earthly Branches is associated with a birth magnetic orientation. Each birth magnetic orientation, in turn, has its own compatible orientations. In deciding whether a door should be installed in the middle, to the left, or to the right, I rely on the directional flow of water spirit chi. An understanding of these two methods, the principal tools in door positioning, is knowledge that any geomancer must possess.

11. The Destructive Energy of a Road Pointing at a Site

When I first arrived in the United States, I resided for some time in the city of Tukwila in the State of Washington. While staying there I noticed a store located at the western end of Strander, the town's main street. This store frequently changed names and had a new owner virtually every month. A "Closed" sign often hung on the door while remodeling took place inside. I was told that this store, located at the end of the road, had undergone twelve different owners in one year. After observing the store and surrounding road patterns, I noticed the classic case of a site being targeted by the destructive energy of an oncoming road.

Strander is a long, straight road with heavy traffic, and the store is located right at the end of this road. The many cars traveling along the street carry with them wave after wave of chi directly aimed at the store. Inside the store, the surging chi is turbulent and unstable. Whatever the business established, the owner would eventually decamp and take flight.

Americans who did not understand feng-shui were puzzled by the fact that so many businesses had failed at this location.

In Honolulu, I was shocked to learn that Mitsukoshi, a large,

Japanese-owned department store, had lost its business and closed down. When I took a look, it turned out that this was another case of a site being targeted by the formidable destructive energy of a long, straight, oncoming road.

A house targeted by an oncoming road is analogous to an animal with arrows flying straight towards it. In this feng-shui pattern, known as "arrow piercing heart," it is difficult to keep malevolent energy in check. People with the special ability to observe chi can see the endless agitation of earth chi at such a site; and people living inside such houses are like little dinghies rocking amidst stormy, turbulent waves.

Oftentimes, people living in such houses are very temperamental and accidental deaths, suicides, or homicides may result. If commercial property is built upon the site, then there are often difficulties in making money.

Some people propose erecting a large wall at the end of an onrushing road to ward off destructive energy. They advocate that this be done before any houses are built on the other side of the wall. This building of this dam-like structure is one solution, but would such a large wall at the end of a road not disrupt the aesthetic appearance of the street?

Others have also proposed that the buildings at such sites be designed as circular structures, similar to the designs of some large hotels. This is also a workable solution since cylindrical buildings can indeed minimize the agitation of onrushing chi caused by the approaching road. This is done by dividing and diverting the noxious chi into two streams that flow away to the left and right.

Taoist Master Ch'ing Chen has told me, "The method for common households to counteract the onslaught of energy from a road is to install a semicircular pool in the front yard, with the outside curve facing the oncoming road, and the pool always 80% filled with water." This employs the curvature of a semi-circle to ward off the onrushing sha-chi. The water also neutralizes this sha-chi, and residents of the house can thus keep their peace.

Some geomancers have taught people to hang objects such as concave mirrors, bronze bells, or flutes as remedies, but these objects do not have that great a resolving power and can only provide a limited measure of psychological relief.

If one is to build a large structure at the end of an onrushing road, such a structure can be a temple, as the round pillars of a temple can divert and minimize sha-chi from the road. A courthouse or other government buildings that incorporate cylindrical structures into its designs (such as the round columns in front of the White House) are also good solutions. If, in front of the courthouse, city hall, or temple, one adds a fountain, the site is even safer. Fountains are uniquely useful in these situations.

A man asked me what one should do if one's house is at the end of an oncoming road but not enough land is available for one to install a semicircular pond. When I asked him if he could move, he replied that it was not financially feasible for him to relocate.

In principle, when I help someone in feng-shui readings, I offer "countermeasure" methods as a first solution. If the problem cannot be resolved this way, then I suggest relocation. If relocation is not feasible, then I teach them to employ "spiritual remedies."

Taoist Master Ch'ing Chen has instructed, "Find a piece of green bamboo and, after removing the green peel, draw on it a talisman that stops sha-chi from onrushing roads. Select a date marked as 'Ting' on the lunar calendar and bury the talisman in the ground in front of the house." Such a remedy offers a "spiritual solution" to a feng-shui problem.

In my opinion, feng-shui deals specifically with patterns and flow of chi and energy in the land. Both residential and burial site feng-shui are affected by earth chi. Since the elements of feng-shui are a part of nature, one should avoid extensive human interference in changing a site's feng-shui.

As for the "spiritual remedies," they are Taoist solutions that fall under the heading of "shamanistic" or "magical practices" and are separate from general feng-shui knowledge. I, Living Buddha Lian-sheng, understand general feng-shui as well as the Taoist magical practices. This is because feng-shui, the pattern and flow of energy in the land, is inherently the manifestations of yin and yang and the five elements; esoteric and magical practices can thus balance the elements and harmonize yin and yang.

Most geomancers are aware of the adverse patterns of oncoming roads, but opinions differ on how to remedy the situation. The remedies disclosed here are invaluable.

12. Adverse Conditions "Outside" and "Inside" the Door

When taking a feng-shui reading for a house, one first determines the orientation. Next, one must note whether or not there are any "outside" or "inside" adverse conditions.

The following outside conditions are to be avoided when they directly face one's door:

— Electric poles or large pillars

— A long and straight onrushing main road

— Deep pits or a broken cliff very close to the house

— The curve of a road, river, or building that points at one's house

— Chimney, corner, "knife-edge," or other sharp and pointed objects projecting from the house across the street

— The front door of another house if it is larger than one's own front door

— Manure pit, vegetable patch, garbage incinerator or any filthy objects

All these are unfavorable outside conditions that should be avoided. While some of the above factors have an effect directly on the "earth chi," others are primarily psychological. If the adverse influence is due to earth chi, then we have to use remedies that can change the earth chi.

If the adverse influence is psychological, then we have to resort to "psychological remedies." For example, some people write words such as "bring me money" on an electric pole as a symbolic psychological relief. They go outdoors, see the pole and read the phrase "bring me money." Over time, the psychological block caused by the electric pole will be removed.

Some people feel psychologically better by hanging certain objects outside their front doors. These include "pa-k'uas (eight trigrams)," mirrors, talismans, flutes, and bells. "Pa-k'uas" are used to neutralize noxious sha-chi, mirrors are reflectors and enhancers, talismans destroy evil spirits, flutes (which in Chinese sounds the same as the word "whittle") whittle down the inauspicious and ominous, and bells avert evil influences.

This mindset of self-protection is understandable, so we need not berate people who, by hanging such objects, seek to receive some psychological comfort. In fact, these psychological relief methods do work to a certain degree and, if they can be employed in combination with rituals and the "intent to invoke divine protection," they form a kind of magical practice.

However, there are situations wherein psychological relief methods will not work. Some examples are when the house is facing a large deep pit, an onrushing road, a manure pit, or when it is situated right outside the bow of a curve. In such cases, before the psychological relief methods could avert the negative influences from the earth chi, one's household would have already been stricken by natural or man-made disasters.

The following inside conditions are to be avoided when they occur directly inside the front door:

— Facing a staircase upon entering

— Face a "knife-edge" (which is the corner of a wall in line with the mid-point of the front door)

— Facing a beam which points at one

— A wall that is so close that one can hardly turn around

— Any of the following visible upon entering the front door: a bed in a bedroom; a fire in the kitchen; the toilet in a bathroom; a fireplace

— The back door. When the house has its front door connected to the back door this way, it is known as "having its chest pierced."

— Such a narrow construction that the front and back of the house are too close. Such construction is known as "having a compressed chest"

There are reasons why such conditions are undesirable. For example, in the case where the front door leads directly to the back door, the chi slips away as soon as it enters the door. Here the chi cannot be stored. When a house is unable to store chi, the people living there will have financial problems.

When chi enters the door and is stopped by a staircase or a wall that is too close, or if the space between the front and back of the house is too narrow, the chi will become chaotic. Families living in houses with such designs will not get rich and will experience disharmony.

As soon as chi enters the door and faces a "knife-edge," or a directly pointing beam, bed, fire, or toilet, then people living in the house will become agitated, hot-tempered, accident-prone, inflicted by illnesses or strange diseases. Their children also will suffer these ailments.

I, Living Buddha Lian-sheng, feel that the front door is a major chi entrance, as well as the portal through which people come and go. As such, it has an extremely significant role in affecting the fortune of the whole house. One should pay special attention to the conditions inside as well as outside the front door, and should avoid all destructive features. Otherwise, even if the house is designed to be auspiciously oriented, the existence of adverse conditions will ensure that one's fortunes will come to nothing.

Ideally, treatments for a house with adverse conditions existing inside or outside the front door include alterations that will remove the offensive features. True geomancers are able to employ simple altering methods to rectify the situations. These achieve better results than resorting to the hanging of objects that provide mainly psychological relief.

The treatment for a house with adverse conditions outside the front door is to change the position of front door to an orientation that does not have the destructive conditions but that is still compatible with the birth magnetic orientation of the head of the household.

To treat the adverse conditions inside the front door, one can remodel or relocate the offensive feature.

Regarding the size of the front door, it should be entirely determined by the size of the house itself. Both a large house with a small door or a small house with a large door are inappropriate. Fire, toilets, and filthy objects either outside or inside must absolutely be avoided as they adversely affect the health and harmony of the family living in the house.

13. The Money-Reserve Spot is the Chi-Gathering Spot

I once evaluated the feng-shui of a rich man's new home. Although a self-proclaimed master in the art of residential feng-shui had designed many elements of his new house, I found many of the designs riddled with errors. I could not help but mentally note the ineptitude of this individual who had fanned his reputation through advertisements.

As the rich man walked me through his new house, parading the original designs and his collection of antiques and wealth, I discovered that this luxurious garden villa was missing its "money-reserve spot." The nook where the "money-reserve spot" should have been located had been turned into a passageway.

The rich man said to me, "The person I hired to design this villa is a world class geomancer. His name is often in newspapers, he gives feng-shui talks on television, and he has numerous students."

"Then why did you invite me here?" I said smiling.

He replied, "Because you, Living Buddha Lian-sheng, have the faculty of dharma eyes and can tell whether these designs are any good by simply taking a look around. And, of course, it is also a great honor just to have the Living Buddha shine some light upon this house."

"Well," I said, "would you like to hear the truth or not?"

"Is there something wrong?" he asked astonished.

"Close this passageway…" I began as I pointed out to him the areas that needed to be corrected.

The rich man was stunned. He had not expected his house, specially designed by a renowned feng-shui master, to be filled with so many errors. He did not say a word. As I looked at his dejected mien, I realized I had spoken out of turn.

This rich man chose not to follow my suggestions to make the necessary changes. After all, the original designer was a feng-shui master who often appeared on television….

Approximately one year later…

The same rich man was in his kitchen one day when he suddenly decided to slice some fruit for his guests. He was using a very sharp knife and the knife slipped, severing one of his fingers.

Some time later, he ran for the legislative assembly but failed to be elected.

In another incident, the car he was driving accidentally hit and killed two elementary school students coming out of the local school.

Five of the six factories he owned shut down.

Finally, the rich man called me, "Living Buddha, you were right. It has only been one year and I am finished. The so-called master was a phony and he is still deceiving others!"

Today, I write this book, *Household Feng-shui*, because I wish people to have some knowledge about the workings of earth chi. I hope they will not be fooled and hurt by the many fraudulent feng-shui masters.

After examining the conditions outside and inside the front door, one next must determine where the "money-reserve spot" is.

The money-reserve spot is located at the corner diagonally across from the living room entrance. If the living room door is on the left side, then the money-reserve spot is the "kitty corner" on the right. If the door is on the right side, then the money-reserve spot is the kitty corner on the left. If, however, the living room entrance is in the middle, then both the left and right corners of the opposite wall are money-reserve spots.

The money-reserve spot in a house is the spot most able to easily gather and store chi. The chi here is not the "dead chi" found in storerooms but "live chi" that continually flows into the spot and accumulates. It is a vibrant, circulating chi. In other words, at the money-reserve spot, chi flows in, accumulates, and gradually flows out.

At this money-reserve spot, there should be no windows, doors, or passageways, and it is best that no one walks around that area. It is a nook, a corner formed by two walls.

At the money-reserve spot, it is best to place an evergreen houseplant such as a Japanese rohdea, kapok, palm trees, rubber trees, etc… These plants symbolize vitality, vibrancy, and growth, and thus promote auspiciousness.

It is also a wonderful idea to place a fish bowl with golden fish at the money-reserve spot. Golden fish symbolize gold and wealth, and the word for fish in Chinese rhymes with the word for "leftover" or "reserve." A bowl with live fish located at the money-reserve spot also enhances vivaciousness and the thinking power of the owner. Furthermore, a fish bowl at the money-reserve spot prevents visitors from stepping upon that location.

If there is a French window at the money-reserve spot, chi will slip away. Similarly, if there is a door or passageway, chi also will not gather there. In these situations, wealth will be diluted and money will be lost.

If the money-reserve spot is handled and decorated appropriately, one's luck will steadily rise and produce extremely beneficial profits. By locating the money-reserve spot and giving it the proper attention and decoration, one brings out the most positive features of a home.

The living room is the heart of a house and should not be too gloomy or too bright. The spot that gathers chi is the money-reserve spot and, being the center of all affairs, exerts an important control and influence on the house's overall state.

14. A House that Brings Good Health

The relationship between health and feng-shui is a very wide-ranging topic. It will not be possible to cover it entirely in this book, so in this chapter, I will discuss in detail some of the most important secrets.

Listed below are some correlations between certain illnesses and the conditions of a house:

• Tumor Case — examine a house for any asymmetrical, protruding objects

• Surgical Case — look for missing corners, the installation of skylights, and examine the remodeled or rebuilt parts of a house

• Metabolic Illness — pay attention to the position of incinerators and purifying troughs

• Urology Illness — pay attention to the drainage of water from the house to see if there is any blockage

• Mental Illness — pay attention to the placement of beds and shrines

• Ear and Nose Illnesses — pay attention to the positions of windows to see if there are problems in their placements

• Bone Illness — pay attention to horizontal beams and the

structure of pillars

Although it may not seem apparent, a house definitely can influence one's health. Ordinary feng-shui practitioners, perhaps, are unable to point out these intricate connections, but a true master knows that the inhabitants of a house are profoundly influenced by the home in which they live.

First of all, the pathway of chi circulation inside the home will affect its inhabitants.

Secondly, a magnetic field is created when a house is built. The human body itself is also a magnetic field. Whether these two magnetic fields are compatible and harmonize, or whether they repel, is another key factor.

Thirdly, the inhabitants are subjected to the influences of the earth chi or energy from the land upon which the house sits.

I have been studying the positions of bathrooms for some time. The function of a bathroom is actually comparable to that of a purifying trough. If a bathroom is positioned incorrectly, it will predispose the inhabitants to illnesses such as dizziness, eye disease, tooth infections, pneumonia, heart problems, diabetes, gastro-intestinal diseases, hepatitis, and nerve problems.

When we draw a cross at the center of a house and extend the arms of the cross so that it divides the house into four sections, it is very important that a bathroom not be located anywhere along these lines. A bathroom located on the lines of the cross will definitely affect the health of the home's inhabitants.

Incinerators do not refer to stoves in kitchens but to fireplaces, rather common features in American households. Fireplaces are related to hot tempers. It is critical that the fireplace not be placed directly across from the front door, because the sight of fire upon entering the house immediately raises one's temper. This factor plays an important role in causing the kind of disharmony that leads to the break-up of many families. (There is a connection between the high rate of divorce of American couples and the fireplaces in their households.)

Because fireplaces are of the fire element, they should not be positioned on the northern end of the line bisecting a house. This is because the elements of fire and water are incompatible. Neither should a fireplace be placed on the southern end of the middle line bisecting the house because the elements of fire and fire together will be too ferocious.

The best position for fireplaces is the east direction.

Incinerators that can stir hot tempers also should not be placed anywhere along the lines of the cross. Fire can significantly affect one's health, so it is best to locate such a feature at the east, southeast, and northwest positions.

The fire element has the most important role in one's body. Fire is temperature, and all types of inflammation and infection are related to fire. We should install bathrooms and incinerators at positions that will not bring us disasters.

It is also important to pay attention to the water drainage of a house. When water drains smoothly, without any obstruction, decaying matter will not accumulate. Poor drainage will result in bad quality air inside the house and, when the air is poor and smells of mildew, people living in the house will definitely become ill.

Regarding the positions of beds and shrines, these I will discuss in a subsequent chapter.

Another issue to consider is the placement of plants inside and outside the home. In my opinion, both indoor and outdoor plants are valuable, not only for aesthetic reasons, but also for their ability to enhance the vitality of a house, as with the example of having a vibrant plant at the money-reserve spot. Placing a houseplant next to a door or in an unclean location also signifies "purification" and the removal of unlucky and violent matters.

If a dwelling is completely lacking of any surrounding vegetation, it is necessary to plant trees and shrubs outside one's house. On the other hand, trees that are too tall or dense are undesirable because they create a dismal atmosphere. When tall and dense trees block out sunlight, the yin energy of a house increases and becomes inviting to evil spirits and ghosts. Living in a house that produces such gloomy feelings adversely affects one's health.

Windows should be installed based on the principle of providing sufficient air ventilation and optimal sunlight for the house. Too many windows are just as bad as too few. A house that is too bright or too dim is undesirable. If the house is too bright, chi dissipates. If the house is too dim, decaying chi gathers and invites evil spirits.

The most auspicious scenario for a house allows an optimal amount of light and good air circulation. In such a house, air flows slowly through, without obstruction, even through places where chi accumulates. Achieving such a state is a great art.

15. Fire Problems in the Kitchen

A newlywed couple once invited me to their home for a feng-shui consultation. They lived in a very beautiful home surrounded by trees with red blossoms and berries. While inspecting the kitchen, I realized that the position of the stove presented a problem. Their "designer" home had the stove built right in the center of the kitchen. It stood in the middle of the room, unshielded by any objects. Furthermore, the faucet and basin were located directly across from the stove.

Such a placement is problematic for two reasons:

1) It is important that the kitchen fire be located in a place that gathers chi. Only a fire that gathers chi can continually burn and maintain its temperature. According to the book *The Secrets of Earth Magic*, a stove should be protected on three sides with chi flowing in from the fourth side. The best locations for stoves are the south, east, or southeast positions.

Although an unshielded stove located in a central island is a convenient working area, it does not afford the advantage of easily storing chi. Quick dissipation of the temperature of the stove fire can lead to the dissipation of money.

2) It is disastrous to have the kitchen faucet directly facing the stove fire, as this symbolizes the clashing of fire and water.

From my observations, such a design portends great trouble and can lead to sexual promiscuity and excessive drinking.

Upon arrival, I noticed that the mistress of the house was a very beautiful, graceful lady with tapering fingers and soft palms. Her shoulders were round and her back not too thin. In terms of physiognomy, the upper, middle, and lower segments of her face were well proportioned. She had the hallmark features of a distinguished woman. But I also noticed a coquettishness in her bright, almond-shaped eyes and a charming seductiveness in the way she moved and swayed—characteristics of someone with "secret peach-blossom luck." (The term "peach-blossom luck" in Chinese refers to the luck one has in attracting lovers.)

I asked my friend, "Do the newlyweds believe in feng-shui?"

The mutual friend who had invited me said, "Only a little. They work in scientific fields."

"Then the purpose for my coming today was...?" I asked.

"Just to get acquainted with them and take a look around," answered my friend.

Since I was only there to get acquainted and enjoy the home's gorgeous furnishings, I needed to be tactful by commenting only on the good and avoiding mention of anything negative. I wanted the meeting to be harmonious and cheerful, and I did not want my friends to feel any unpleasantness in the air.

It was only after leaving the house that I told my friend to give a message to the owners: they must rectify the fire problem in the kitchen.

The owners ignored my advice.

A year later, I learned that the lady of the house had had an extramarital affair with her supervisor at work, and her husband had a mistress and had become an alcoholic. In the end, the marriage ended and each went their separate ways.

I would like everyone to heed this fact: if the "kitchen fire" is situated in the center of the kitchen, then whichever direction the faucet is installed in—north, south, east, or west—chances are that it will be sitting directly across from the stove fire. With the faucet a symbol for "yang" and the stove a symbol for "yin," this is an omen for licentiousness and promiscuity.

I have noticed that the designer kitchens of many new homes in the United States have stoves built right in the middle of the kitchens. Architects of such kitchen designs are definitely uninformed in the science of feng-shui. Although their goal may be to create a convenient, aesthetic space, they are, however, contributing to the flourishing of licentiousness!

I want readers to know that, when one enters a house, fire must not be the first thing one sees. This means that the kitchen or the fireplace should not be the first thing seen upon entering a home. Avoid having these two types of "fire chi" facing the front door.

In business settings, such as restaurants, under no circumstances should stoves (gas stoves, water heaters, electric stoves, electric cookers, etc.) be installed at the center of the cross of the restaurant. Such centrally located "fire chi" can pollute the air inside the entire restaurant, creating a hot and fiery atmosphere. In such an environment, business partners will not get along and customers will not feel comfortable. Over time, they will not want to set foot in the restaurant. And even more importantly, "fire chi" in the center makes it difficult for earth chi to remain balanced.

In the kitchen, one must also pay attention to the following things: Make sure garbage does not accumulate, is well contained, sealed, and frequently disposed of. Pay attention to the flow of water in the kitchen sink. Also, select a stove fan that does not have its working parts exposed, and install a range hood that does not protrude too conspicuously as this also affects kitchen feng-shui. Finally, one must not install skylights in kitchens as this is conducive to the upward spreading of "fire chi." A skylight opening in the kitchen incurs unexpected accidents and calamities.

16. Desks in Offices and Studies

A medical doctor once consulted a famous geomancer for help in positioning a desk in his office. As soon as the geomancer arrived, the first words out of his mouth were the fees for his service. "The total charge will be three thousand U.S. dollars!" said the feng-shui master.

"Three thousand U.S. dollars for one desk?" the medical doctor asked flabbergasted.

"Yes," replied the geomancer. "One thousand for determining the orientation, one thousand for selecting an auspicious date, and one more thousand for personally moving the desk for you. All together, it will be three thousand U.S. dollars."

The doctor opened his mouth to speak, but could think of nothing to say. Finally he said, "I think I will just consult someone else instead."

"Whom do you have in mind?"

"There is a Living Buddha Lian-sheng, Sheng-yen Lu, who never demands a price for his consultations and lets people pay as they like."

The geomancer's face turned ashen, and he went off in a

huff.

This is a true story in which the setting up of a desk would have cost an individual three thousand dollars. If readers carefully study this short chapter, they can learn how to set up their own business or study desks and save themselves three thousand U.S. dollars! Such knowledge is definitely worth learning.

The theories and principles behind the arranging of all desks are the same, whether in one's workplace or in one's study room at home. Essentially, one must remember the following six principles:

1) Avoid facing the door directly — Do not position one's desk or chair in the line of the doorway. That is, when a perpendicular line is drawn from the door, the desk and chair should not be in the path of this line. If they are, onrushing chi charging through the door will cause one to feel restless and agitated.

2) Avoid sitting with one's back to the door — From our sitting positions, we should be able to see people entering and exiting the room. We feel insecure if we cannot see people coming or going, and sitting with our backs to the door encourages mean-spirited people to act behind our backs. One's career will also lose momentum, leaving one dispirited and listless. Over time, one's situation will decline and worsen.

3) Have a solid wall behind one — When sitting at the desk, avoid having windows directly behind the chair. I often see people sitting before large French windows which are actually not strong or solid enough to lend sufficient support. To sit in a chair in front of a large window is to sit insecurely on shaky ground. When earth chi travels to that spot, it slips away and, as a result, we receive no help from the earth energy.

4) The back support should be close — In addition to having a strong, solid wall behind the chair, the wall should be

close to the chair in order to provide adequate support. In the past I have come across leaders of large companies who, for the sake of showing off their wealth and enterprise, purchased extra large desks and plunked them down in the middle of their offices. On top of their desks were twenty telephones used to conduct international business. Unfortunately, with their desks so far away from proper back support, they also will not get help from the earth energy.

5) Utilize the twelve Earth Branches directions as a guide for orientation — Once one's desk faces the door, does not sit in the pathway of a door, and has a solid and close wall behind it, the next step is to use a geomancer's compass to determine the two orientations that have a mutually attractive relationship with the magnetic orientation of the user of the desk. If neither of the two orientations will work, one may pick an orientation that is neutral. This way, one can still avoid loss of earth energy. Ideally, of course, it is best if all requisites are met, and the desk faces the optimal orientation.

6) Selection of date — one may consult a lunar calendar to select either a "Ting" or "Man" day to move and set up the desk.

Why is the proper arrangement of an office or study desk so important? The reasons are very simple. When one works or studies at such a desk, one finds one has more energy and is more excited about work or study. One's memory becomes sharper, and one is more relaxed, happy, and efficient. With a desk positioned at a good spot, one is able to tap into the earth energy, and this helps everything proceed harmoniously. One's work will advance by leaps and bounds.

If the office or study desk is not well placed and the magnetic orientation of the desk and one's own magnetic orientation repel, one will not have sufficient energy to carry out one's work, even if one was initially enthusiastic. Instead, mistakes will be made. Fatigue will overwhelm one. One's situation will worsen and it will be difficult to rebound.

When I perform household feng-shui readings, I pay particular attention to the desk in the study. Desk placement is equally important for children. It greatly influences whether or not a child likes to study, and whether or not he or she gets good grades.

I once visited the home of a physicist with a Ph.D. degree. I asked him, "How many years have you not been sitting at your desk?"

"How did you know?"

"This desk sits directly in the pathway of a door. How can one sit here long? Besides, dust and spider webs have accumulated behind the chair, which tell me this chair has long been deserted."

"Is this feng-shui?"

"No, this is not feng-shui. This is meticulous observation," I replied.

17. Staircases Can Be Destructive

Large western-style luxury homes often have a staircase in the center of the living room, with the front door opening directly into this room. The pillars of the staircase are often highly decorated with ornate carvings. Perhaps, for many, the staircase itself has become an ornamental piece. Some of these staircases are spiral-shaped and very beautiful. What a picture perfect scene it is for arriving visitors to be greeted by the host or hostess walking elegantly down a spiral staircase.

Many more examples, in which the staircase directly faces the front door, can be found in western-style homes.

The importance of staircases has been overlooked by some geomancers. Some geomancers are of the opinion that, upon entry, seeing a staircase leading up to a second story signifies a "successive ascent." Conversely, they believe that entering a house and seeing a staircase leading down to the basement is unlucky because it signifies "a successive descent."

In fact, this concept is erroneous. When chi enters the front door and encounters a flight of stairs, the horizontal edges of each step cut and disrupt its flow. Chi entering the house is thrown into chaos and unable to remain calm and smooth.

In geomancy, the sight of a staircase upon entry through the front door signifies "a rough and bumpy road." It denotes "unexpected destruction" and is a very serious matter. In my opinion, seeing a staircase when walking into a house is similar to seeing a pillar when one walks out of the house—both have the same powerful destructive force.

The staircases found in the living rooms of large, luxury homes are actually symbols of "decline." In ordinary homes, the sight of a staircase upon entry is actually a symbol of "the occurrence of accidents."

I once inspected the feng-shui of a home in which the family members had been involved in over ten car accidents within one year. In some instances, their cars had rammed into others' cars. Other times, their cars were the ones hit. In one incident, the gears of their parked car slipped and their car hit another car.

On one occasion when a month had passed in which no accidents occurred, the family decided to rejoice and go out to celebrate. Upon backing the car out of the garage, however, they hit their own garage door, denting their vehicle and damaging the garage door. Although no one had been injured, they suffered another incident of unexpected financial losses.

The owner of the house told me that all the drivers in the family were cautions drivers with more than ten years of driving experience. But, for some strange reason, every month someone would get into an accident. "If this continues," he said, "we're all going to have nervous breakdowns! Our family is developing 'car-phobia,' and it's as if a curse has been placed upon us."

Upon inspecting their situation, I realized that their problems resulted from "the sighting of a staircase upon entering the door." The door and staircase directly faced each other. In addition, the flight of stairs was located directly upon the northeast position known in geomancy as "the ghost door." Geomancers have misgivings about this northeast "ghost door" position and avoid installing staircases or elevators there.

After my inspection, they remodeled the house and removed the phenomenon of "seeing the staircase when entering the door." Since then, this family has been able to enjoy a peaceful life without mishaps.

In Taiwan, during my feng-shui inspections, I had seen a kind of steel staircase that, due to space constraints, was spiral shaped and looked like a steel column. It was very inconvenient as it only allowed one person to go up or down at a time. Such staircases, if installed at inappropriate positions, can be particularly destructive.

There are three ways to modify staircases:

1) Change the position — If a staircase directly faces the front door, change its position. The key is this: avoid seeing any flight of stairs from the front door to ensure that the steps will not slice the entering chi.

2) Hide the staircase — If one is building a new house, it is best to design a staircase that is "hidden" because staircases only have destructive influences and no positive influences. In designing new homes, it is a good idea to hide staircases behind walls. An even better idea is to have the staircase flanked by two walls and concealed behind a door. This way, the steps are not seen and the space beneath the staircase can be used as a storeroom or washroom.

3) Cover the staircase — In a house that is already built, it is probably very difficult to move a staircase that directly faces the front door. In such cases, one must resort to the method of covering the flight of stairs by placing a screen halfway between the staircase and the front door. One may even hang a mirror on the screen to enhance the depth of the space in the entryway, so that one will not feel oppressed by the shortened

distance. This way, the flight of stairs is not seen upon entry, and one only needs to walk around the screen to go upstairs. Additionally, one can also use the mirror to check one's appearance before going out.

As for the hanging of chime bells, flutes, or bronze nails, these techniques only bring limited psychological comfort and have little practical benefit. As chi enters the door and encounters the flight of stairs, it will still become chaotic.

What about staircases outside the front door?

If one has to climb a flight of stairs to reach one's front door, then such a staircase is fine. If one must walk down a flight of stairs to reach the door of one's home, then attention must be paid to ensure that the distance between the stairwell and door is not too close or confining.

These are the keys to the positioning of staircases.

18. The Haunted Antiques

I once traveled to San Francisco to inspect the feng-shui of a rich family's home.

The owner loved collecting antiques. From the stone lions outside his front door to his living room and bedrooms, antiques were everywhere. His collection included Buddhist statues, porcelain vases, bowls, and vessels. Jade stone sculptures of birds and beasts, antique paintings, ancient objects, such as desks and chairs, horizontal inscribed boards, cooking utensils, and even articles of clothing and beds used by the ancients filled his home.

In fact, what began as a fondness for antiques had grown into an obsession. He had even purchased and displayed in his house ancient ancestor tablets that others had worshipped.

Then, strange things started happening.

During that year, the owner would often feel a feverish sensation on his forehead and a strange fishy taste in his mouth. He tired easily and was often irascible and moody.

His wife often saw black shadows. Sometimes they walked from one room to another, and other times, they sat next to her on the sofa. She even saw these shadows in her sleep, and strange noises would often alarm and wake her at night. She had not had a good night's sleep in a long while. She sensed that she was surrounded by harmful ghosts and began to lose interest in life as a depression settled over her.

Their daughter, who lived at home, was a Catholic and had always been very well-behaved. Recently, however, her behavior had drastically changed. She was attacked by frequent dizzy spells and started smoking and drinking. She derided and taunted her parents and often came home seething with anger and hatred. She acted unusually wild, and it appeared as if she had become a completely different person.

Family members were constantly sick with illnesses such as red, swelling allergic skin breakouts, vomiting, and diarrhea that alternated with constipation. Their stomachs felt bloated and uncomfortable, their muscles and bodies ached, and they lost all appetite for food. The family had all gone to see doctors, but no one was able to diagnose or cure their illnesses.

The family then consulted several feng-shui masters in San Francisco. They were told their house had bad feng-shui. Following the advice of these geomancers, they made several changes in their home, but none resulted in any improvement in their lives.

Of course, when I arrived at their huge mansion, I also found a few flaws with the feng-shui. But after a careful inspection, I discovered that their problems were not caused by the adverse influences of unfavorable feng-shui, but by the antiques in the home. Among the huge collection, three pieces had "spiritual energies" attached to them.

The first object was a vat with a large body and small opening originated from Yunan, China. This vat was once used as a container for storing "poisonous worms" employed in black magic. The spiritual energy from the worms remained in the vat and could still cause mischief today.

The second object was armor worn by an ancient European warrior. After its owner had been murdered, his spirit attached to the armor, giving it a "spiritual energy." On the anniversary dates of his murder, the power of his energy would augment, giving rise to "haunted house" phenomena.

The third object was a stone tablet from an ancient Chinese monastery that had been used in memorial services. After purchasing it, the owner had displayed it in his living room. Although the memorial tablet was very old, the spiritual energies gathered there had not yet dispersed and could also cause mischief.

After explaining the situation, the mistress of the house then told me, "In my dreams, snakes and worms bite and crawl all over me every night. It is so nauseating. Every night I fight with these crawlers until morning. Several times at dusk, I have even seen the shadow of a tall, heroic-looking warrior. All this is in addition to the many strange shadows I see around the house. It is all just so terrifying."

Both the owner and his wife begged me, "You must help us."

So I put a "restraint mantra" on each of the three antique objects. I also instructed them to take the three pieces to an antique shop for a cheap consignment sale.

Later I learned that after removing these three antiques from their home, they were cured of all their "strange illnesses."

In the past, I have come across quite a few of these cases in my feng-shui consultation. Many rich people have carelessly bought antiques with spirits attached to them. It is true that displaying these antique objects may enhance the grandeur of a home, but it does not pay if these objects have attached spiritual energies and bring on haunted phenomena.

Therefore, in the acquisition of antiques to be displayed in one's living room, one should first be acquainted with the origin of these antiques. Were they used in memorial rituals? Did they come from temples or monasteries? What was the relationship between the antique and its owner? What are the words written on the artifacts? Are they burial objects from an ancient tomb? Are there images of gods or Buddhas on the objects? These are very important questions. Essentially, attached negative spiritual energy causes disturbances in the magnetic field of one's home, engendering mischievous phenomena.

I, Living Buddha Lian-sheng, consider wood or stone sculptures with images of deities, men, or animals to be possible lodgings for spirits. Such wood or stone objects with attached spirits may display haunted phenomena of varying magnitudes.

This chapter is beyond the scope of feng-shui, but it also illustrates some of the evil phenomena existing beyond an ordinary individual's perception.

19. Selecting the Master Bedroom

When selecting a room to serve as the master bedroom in a house, most geomancers will either choose the main room on the "dragon side" or simply pick the largest, most luxurious room to be the master bedroom. It is not uncommon for people ignorant of feng-shui to make this same decision.

This selection is not necessarily wrong. However, an expert geomancer will go one step further to ensure that the master bedroom is the room with the greatest vigorous energy. Such a room is not always located on the upper dragon side and not necessarily the largest room. Such a room could be a relatively smaller, simpler room.

I once inspected the home of a movie actress and advised her to move out of her own huge, elegant bedroom and into a maid's room. How different those two rooms were!

"Why should I switch rooms?" she asked.

"Though your current bedroom is large, the chi in the room is weak and insufficient. Though small, the maid's room, on the other hand, has very nurturing, vibrant chi. If you believe me, give this new room a try."

The actress followed my advice and moved into the maid's room to sleep.

In less than three months, she was cast as the female lead in a feature film. Her performance garnered much critical acclaim, rocketing her to stardom. She began receiving so many movie offers that she could not attend to them all. During that period of time, daily newspaper articles praised her acting skills. She indeed became a red-hot movie star. She had one secret, however, which was that, every night, she abandoned her luxurious bedroom to sleep in the maid's room.

Perhaps some will think that, as the founder of a religious school, Living Buddha Lian-sheng's bedroom must be the upper room on the dragon side and the largest room in his house. It is true that my house has an upper room on the dragon side that is also the largest room in the house, but this room is not my bedroom.

I stay in a small room located at the "tail end of the tiger side." This small room has one door and one window looking out into the backyard. And though this room is small, it accumulates and stores a vibrant energy. Such a room is the true master bedroom in the house. It is this room that enables me to develop my potential energy and sustain an indomitable will.

If a large and luxurious upper room gathers the strongest, most nourishing earth chi, one of course should use it as the master bedroom. The thing one must then heed is the placement of windows. Oversized French windows often lead to the dissipation and weakening of nourishing chi. Lighting and windows are important determinants as to whether a master bedroom gathers or dissipates chi.

In fact, the chi in bedrooms often impacts one's descendants as well. Weak chi, lacking in essence of affection, indicates few or no offspring. Accumulating chi, the presence of essence of affection, reflects plentiful offspring. If one wonders whether the offspring will be sons or daughters, make the following careful inspections: a bedroom with more yang chi than yin chi predisposes the family to the birth of sons; a bedroom with more yin chi than yang chi predisposes the family to the birth of daughters. When yang and yin chi are present in equal amounts, there is an equal chance of having sons or daughters.

As for the influences of bedroom chi upon one's career, accumulating, vigorous chi indicates success. Conversely, weak chi portends decline and failure.

The height of the bedroom ceiling is also very important. Ceilings that are too low cause one to feel crushed and suppressed. It is a pity that some wealthy folk deliberately install bumpy, uneven decorations, such as lavish canopies, on ceilings directly above their beds. Such adornments may initially appear elegant, but over time, they become boring and oppressing. Low ceilings, marks of disaster, symbolize the "suffocation" of one's career!

High bedroom ceilings should be avoided as well. Such rooms lack an essence of affection and have cold, unwelcoming atmospheres. One way to counteract this, when no other remedy exists, is to paint the ceiling a warmer, darker color.

Some people like to hang mirrors in their bedrooms. Mirrors serve two purposes: they enhance the depth of a room, and they repel things. In general, geomancers advise using mirrors in bedrooms sparingly.

Used appropriately, mirrors can convey a sense of calm and happiness. They can also contribute positively to the spiritual dimension or create "magic" in one's life. Such objectives, however, require the service of a truly learned teacher.

Truly learned geomancers have the ability to determine which room in a house is the true master bedroom. They can also discern the connection of each bedroom to its occupants. For the average individual, the least one can do is to sleep in a bedroom one finds "peaceful."

20. Rules for Positioning Beds

Page 79 in my book *Ti Ling Hsien Tsung* [Earth Magic and Spirit] begins the chapter "The Placement of Beds" where I recorded Taoist Master Ch'ing Chen's following instructions:

Avoid having a strong beam pressing down on the bed.

Be able to see the door when lying in bed.

Avoid having the bed directly facing the door.

In this chapter, I shall explain these rules in detail.

1) Avoid having a strong beam pressing down on the bed.

Above the bed, there should not be any steel reinforced concrete beams, transverse or parallel. Wooden beams are not good either. Pipes for air conditioning or heating should also be avoided. It is also not good to have beds under staircases. In brief, it is best not to have anything directly above the bed. Deliberately installing canopy-type decorations above one's bed invites trouble. Once the feeling of oppression is generated, ill influences result.

2) Be able to see the door when lying in bed.

When we are lying in bed, we must be able to see the bedroom door. The bed is in a correct orientation when we are able to see the door without straining or contorting. Some people place the head of the bed against the wall that has the door, and when they sleep, they face away from the door. This is an incorrect orientation. Sleeping with one's back to the door has ill effects on one's health.

3) Avoid having the bed directly facing the door.

When a bed faces the door, chi entering the room rushes straight toward the bed. The best position for the head of a bed is the corner diagonal from the door. It is ominous to place a bed directly facing the door. When chi first enters a room, it has not yet settled down and such strong chi can be harmful.

I would like to add a few more points. Firstly, do not arbitrarily install skylights in the ceiling above the bed. Secondly, the head of the bed must rest against a solid wall. The wall against which the bed leans should not have a window directly above the head of the bed. To rest against a solid wall is to have support. Sleeping in a bed directly under a window may have ill influences on one's health and wealth.

I once performed a feng-shui reading for a household whose family members all slept in beds placed in the center of their rooms. This kind of placement is inappropriate. Without walls for support, one feels "insubstantial," as if one is "floating in the air." Such bed placement will in fact lead a person's career to become ungrounded and "insubstantial".

Is it also necessary to orient the bed according to one's magnetic birth orientation (based on the twelve Earth Branches directions)? I have already addressed this in the book *Ti Ling Hsien Tsung*. The ideal situation is for the main door of one's home to be in an orientation compatible with the magnetic birth orientation of the owner and for the bed to also be oriented appropriately following the twelve Earth Branches directions. However, due to the constraints in the rules for positioning a bed, it is often impossible to orient the bed according to the twelve Earth Branches directions. Therefore, in this situation, I feel that one does not have to adhere rigidly to these particular positioning rules. There are many other reasons as well.

I previously stated the following: "Some geomancers believe they must take the magnetic birth orientation into account in positioning the bed. The result is an awkward looking, ill-placed bed with unusable working space. It is irrational to sleep in such a bed. A bed positioned so that its four sides are facing corners may even invite noxious chi, grave injuries, and possible death. It is therefore erroneous to claim that one must always orient the bed according to one's magnetic birth orientation."

I have, for example, seen quite a few unusual bedrooms:

1) One had mirrors installed all around, above, and below the bed. The room felt like an illusory dreamland of mirrors.

2) In another, the headboard of the bed was a dragon sculpture that spewed water.

3) Installed on all sides of another bed were heads of animals such as tigers, leopards, lions, and elephants. Sleeping in such a bed must make one feel like the king of beasts!

4) I once saw a heart-shaped bed, whose owner treasured love above all else.

5) Another individual had a round bed, placed in the center of the bedroom.

6) One bed had a mechanism installed so it would rock up and down and rotate in both directions.

Unfortunately, all the rich men sleeping in these bedrooms subsequently met their decline. These strange beds were not in accordance with the teachings of feng-shui and symbolized degeneration.

I had heard that some of those beds were actually designed by geomancers to satisfy the psychological needs of their wealthy clients. Yet "too many mirrors" lead to a loss of inspiration. "Water at the head of a bed" indicates entanglements and difficulties. A "bed of animals" causes fatigue in both body and mind. A "heart-shaped bed" can lead to pessimism. "Round beds" make one unfavorable among one's circle of friends. And a "mechanical bed" causes endless disputes. These are the feng-shui implications of the above designs. Such beds may have appealed to the vanities of the wealthy, but the losses incurred were not worth the trouble.

A bed may be comfortable and the room's decorations elegant, yet one should always take feng-shui into consideration. Do not deliberately create strange and unnatural effects. These will lead to sluggishness and confusion as well as the loss of inspiration for work and the diminishing of willpower. One will then become listless, idle, and decadent.

Such are the drawbacks of bedrooms that are too luxurious. Without proper suppression of self-indulgence, endless greed and desire arise.

21. The Placement of Shrines

When I first arrived in the United States, I received many invitations to give feng-shui consultations. One was a request to inspect a "very good" restaurant that had excellent feng-shui. Many geomancers had inspected the locale before me, and they all concurred that the site was very good.

After inspection, I too found the feng-shui very good. However, the reality was that business there was bad. Not only were all the staff sluggish, even patrons appeared to become infected by a miserable dreariness upon entering the restaurant. There were never more than a few customers in the restaurant, and at the time I arrived, the owner could barely afford to pay his bills.

As I looked around the restaurant, I noticed a shrine set up directly above the upper ledge of the door leading from the kitchen into the dining room. This door happened to be the passageway through which waiters brought dishes into the dining room.

I told the owner, "The set up of the shrine is wrong."

"Why is it wrong?"

"There is nothing below the shrine."

"Why is this bad?"

"The shrine is set up with nothing beneath it; this makes it impossible to bring in the money chi. The door below constantly opens and closes, making banging noises. How can a deity sit still at such a spot? This deity ran away a long time ago."

"The deity may have run away, but couldn't the customers have stayed?" the owner said with a laugh.

"The deity running away had a negative influence on business causing customers to also run away."

The owner of the restaurant did not actually believe in the existence of gods or deities, and the installation of a shrine had merely been a customary cultural practice. But after listening to my advice, without further comment, he moved the shrine to a money-reserve spot in the dining room. At the new location, the shrine had solid back support with walls to the right and left preventing chi from slipping away. This new location was also warmer and quieter. I also requested that the owner place a few more lights on the shrine to brighten it and suggested he make regular offerings.

I then told the owner to place an advertisement announcing that, in celebration of the restaurant's first anniversary, each party of customers would receive one complimentary dish and a plate of fruit. I also suggested he hire a new assistant chef to prepare some specialty dishes.

After moving the shrine and following my suggestions, business suddenly turned around. Every day, a long line of customers waited outside. The line stretched from the door all the way to the main road, and inside, the restaurant was always jam-packed. There were so many customers that the owner could hardly believe his good fortune.

Thereafter, each time I visited him, the owner would come out to greet me with a large smile, "Welcome, Living Buddha, my lucky star, welcome."

In this case, by simply moving the shrine from above the kitchen door to an auspicious location where regular offerings were made, the problem was solved. These actions resulted in spiritual protection and prosperity for the entire restaurant.

The owner of the restaurant saw a huge increase in profit and has since opened two additional restaurants. He also consulted me for the remodeling and installing of shrines in these new restaurants. All three restaurants are currently doing very good business and bringing in a great deal of money.

During my feng-shui readings in Taiwan, I remember coming across two shops that also set up shrines directly above passageways. Below the shrines, people walked to and fro. I warned the shop owners against having empty space or traffic below the shrine and suggested they relocate their shrines or close up the passageways. They both said they would do so, yet they never carried out my instructions.

Recently, I learned that one of the owners had declared bankruptcy, and the other was very much in debt and looking for someone to take over the business.

I consider it best not to have any empty space above, below, or on either side of the shrine. If there must be windows in the establishment, these can be installed in the center of the left and right walls. An empty space above or below the shrine is inauspicious because the shrine will not receive money chi. The reason for this is very simple: an opening above, below, or on either side leads to great dissipation of chi and the instability of the chi of the deity.

Even in ordinary households, shrines must be set up in proper locations with no empty space above, below, or on either side. If the shrine is installed correctly, it will accumulate positive energy from the residing deity and compensate for minor feng-shui problems in the home.

In the past, I had written that there should be no empty space above, below, or on either side of the shrine. Many students misunderstood these directions to mean there should be no windows on the three walls. Actually, the only wall that should not have any windows is the wall that forms the shrine's back support. The right and left walls may have windows in the middle as long as these walls still give rise to the form of two "protecting arms."

I have seen cases where shrines were installed beside doors. This is also improper as the opening and closing of the door creates much noise and a draft that leads to unstable chi. Take care to ensure that the back wall of the shrine is strong and solid. If the wall is rickety, the shrine will not sit comfortably and securely. It will eventually fall, and once the shrine falls, bankruptcy will follow.

22. Using the Shrine to Bring in the Water Spirit Chi

S etting up a shrine inside a residential home is tantamount to "tapping into the higher forces of gods and spiritual beings," or the term yung-shen. Put another way, to employ yung-shen is to change a site's existing magnetic field.

Many oriental families traditionally install shrines in their homes to worship and make offerings to the spirits of gods or ancestors. It is true that when one's devotion is sincere, the spirits will respond. However, one must also observe the proper rules when designing the shrine. If the shrine is set up correctly, it will complement one's fortune; conversely, an improperly designed shrine and improper worshipping will bring misfortune. In this regard, caution is warranted.

In judging whether a home will prosper or decline, geomancers should evaluate the house for the presence or absence of the "essence of affection." Its presence leads to prosperity; its absence leads to failure. Proper analysis of the essence of affection, a very intricate, complex subject, demands deep study and training.

How does one determine if the essence of affection exists at one's shrine? The answer lies in the shrine's ability to bring in the "water spirit chi" which carries the essence of affection. "Water spirit" is a collective term that includes rivers, streams, lakes, ditches, oceans, or any other gathering of water vapor. On flatlands, the traveling course of the water spirit is not obvious. However, geomancers have the following definitions: "Mountain" refers to any site at least an inch higher than its surroundings.

"Water" refers to any site at least an inch lower than its surroundings.

Even on relatively flat land, the water spirit can still follow a meandering course.

Listed below are examples of shrines and their relationship to the water spirit and the essence of affection:

1) Outside the bow water — This shrine faces water spirit that forms a curve. The shrine is located outside the curve and is unfavorable.

2) Water spirit from behind — The shrine does not face water spirit which, instead, approaches the shrine from behind. This is unfavorable.

3) Obliquely departing water — This shrine faces water spirit that flows away from the house obliquely. This is unfavorable.

4) Ordinary water — This shrine faces water spirit that flows by in front of the house in a straight course. This is neither good nor bad.

5) Inside the bow water — The shrine faces water spirit that forms a curve cradling the house. This is favorable.

6) Goldfish water — The shrine faces water spirit shaped like the belly of a goldfish. This is favorable.

7) Facing water spirit — The shrine faces water spirit that flows towards the shrine. From the shrine, one must raise one's head to see water flowing from high to low. This is favorable.

8) Side entry water — The shrine faces water spirit flow-

ing in an angle towards the house. This is favorable.

9) Shower water — A tall mountain with a waterfall or stream behind the shrine gives rise to great disasters such as incest or rebellion against superiors.

10) Licentious sounding water — If the shrine faces a river with a blockage that creates turbulence and splashing sounds, this is also greatly disastrous and portends lascivious behaviors.

In brief, the direction the shrine faces may determine whether benevolence or destruction befalls one's home; the type of water spirit faced affects the generation of the essence of affection.

To suppress the noxious or destructive chi associated with water, geomancers learned in the art of yung-shen typically employ the following three talismans:

1) On the first talisman, the following words are inscribed: the Buddha decrees the water to be purified and all noxious chi to be extinguished.

2) On the second talisman, the following words are inscribed: by Heaven's edict received by Master Chang, Master Yang orders the Water Virtue Star to guard this location.

3) And on the third talisman, the following words are inscribed: by Heaven's edict received by Master Chang, Master Yang orders the Sun Water Virtue Tsai-hsun Star to guard this location.

These three talismans were treasures transmitted secretly to me by my master Taoist Master Ch'ing Cheng.

There are many magic practices dealing with water. Among them is the Five Ghosts Method, used primarily to determine whether a residence is favorable or unfavorable. Another method uses the Nine Stars System. (The names of the nine stars are Purity and Truth, Military Pursuits, Destroyer of Armies, Left Supporter, Greedy Wolf, Great Gate, Prosperity,

Scholar, and Right Guardian.) Another method employs the twenty-four mountain positions.

Here is a secret I will share with readers. If there are two different trees of similar size in front of the shrine, two crescent shaped watercourses in front of the shrine, or two crescent shaped watercourses behind the house, this portends that the man of the house will have two wives.

Generally geomancers have many taboos regarding the setting up of shrines. For example, shrines should not be installed under beams, under a staircase, beside passageways, at places concentrated with noxious chi, or in places with frequent foot traffic.

I, Living Buddha Lian-sheng, feel that a shrine bringing in or receiving water spirit chi definitely "has the essence of affection." Some shrines receive the water spirit faster than others because water may be entering from the front, the side, and the back. This is why some people get rich quicker than others do. Wealth may be acquired through proper or legal channels, or through unexpected or ill-gotten means. In some cases, legal money arrives quickly while ill-gotten money arrives slowly; in other cases, the situation is reversed. Only experts can tell whether the wealth will come rapidly or slowly and whether it will come by proper or unexpected channels.

Finally, to relocate a shrine, one must pay attention to these two key factors:

1) Select an auspicious date and hour for the relocation,

2) And invite a Taoist priest or Buddhist monk, nun, or master to perform the ceremony.

23. Old Wells and Water Towers

In Yunling, Taiwan, I once conducted a feng-shui reading for a family living in a western-style building.

Within one year after the owner had moved into this building, three members of his family passed away. One was an elderly individual, but the other two were young people who should not have met such early deaths.

Upon arriving at their home, I first proceeded to the shrine room to pay my respects. I then took a seat in the living room and turned to the owner and asked, "Is there an old well on these grounds?"

"Why yes," the owner replied greatly surprised. "Mr. Lu, you are indeed psychic. We inherited this land from our ancestors, and there indeed was a well. But we had it filled during a previous construction project."

I then told the owner, "Inside the well is the spirit of someone who died there. When you filled the well, you did not perform a Bardo Deliverance service for the soul, and it is now buried inside causing you problems."

"Oh!" the owner was speechless. After a while, he remarked, "I do remember my father telling me a story of a wrongly accused concubine who had jumped into the well. This supposedly occurred during my great grandfather's generation. But Mr. Lu, how did you know about the well?"

"The deity at your shrine told me," I laughed.

"Can you tell me then the actual location of the well?" the owner asked testing me.

"Of course." I stood up and walked over to one of the bathrooms. Pointing inside, I told the owner that the well was underneath the bathroom.

The owner replied, "You have my admiration. You are indeed the best feng-shui master in the world."

Several of my feng-shui students had accompanied me on that trip and are well aware of the details of this "old well incident." To solve the problem, I used the following two spiritual remedies:

1) A ritual was performed to deliver the begrudged soul from the filled well.

2) At the site of the old well, I unearthed a bit of soil and buried a green bamboo inscribed with a talisman for purifying and suppressing noxious chi.

The family living in the building then peacefully resumed their lives.

Old wells play important roles in the feng-shui of residential homes and should not be neglected. In the past, wells, essential to people's livelihood, served as important sources of water and were regarded as key aspects to consider in geomancy surveys. The excavation and closure of wells can significantly affect household feng-shui. Many living creatures, as well as possible spirits, also inhabit old wells.

Old wells can be found not only in Taiwan, but also in modern countries such as the United States. In America, houses built beside lakes or in remote areas far from commercial water suppliers often have wells to draw underground water.

When closing or filling a well, one should obtain a piece of green bamboo, peel off its skin, and inscribe upon it the Earth God Mantra. Select a "Man" date from the lunar calendar to toss the green bamboo into the well. Then one may fill the well with earth. It is better yet if one performs a Bardo Deliverance ceremony prior to the Earth God ritual. This spiritual remedy I learned from my teacher, Taoist Master Ch'ing Chen.

In the United States, to close a well, one can invite a Catholic priest to pray for peace and sprinkle holy water around the mouth of the well before sealing it. The closing of a well is a significant matter that must not be slighted.

Another structure related to underground water is the "water tower." A water tower is often located at the highest point of a building. Being large in size, such a tower naturally protrudes affecting the feng-shui of the entire building. A protruding water tower is difficult to conceal and often creates imbalance or asymmetry in a building.

To avert the water tower's negative influence on feng-shui, I suggest one work on altering the design of the tower. If a water tower is built on the eastern side of a building, then another structure similar in size and shape should be erected on the western side to balance the original protrusion. This structure can be put to many uses and will, at the same time, remove the destructive power of the water tower.

I once inspected a factory where the owners had built a very tall water tower on the tiger side (the north end, in this case) of the factory. After its construction, numerous factory trucks encountered accidents, and the factory suffered great losses. The partners who owned the company began engaging in a power struggle, the morale of staff plummeted, and people loafed during their jobs.

As a solution, I recommended the erection of a second tall water tower, similar in height to the existing one, on the dragon side, the south end of the factory. Strangely, with the completion of the second water tower that restored the building's symmetry, the freight trucks no longer encountered accidents, the efficiency of staff members improved, and the partners began cooperating and working as a team.

Preferably, water towers should be balanced by similar structures and concealed. In this way, the negative forces of water towers can be controlled.

In household feng-shui, geomancers often neglect old wells and water towers. However, their influences are significant, and their locations must be specifically determined.

24. The Inflow and Outflow of Water

In household feng-shui readings, modern geomancers often employ the following systems in their analyses: "Eight Orientations and Twenty-four Mountain Directions," "Four Eastern Life Dwellings and Four Western Life Dwellings," "the Determining of a Favorable Orientation According to the Year of Birth," etc...

For a residence, a yang abode, the most important factor to consider is the site's ability to gather "sheng-chi," or life force. For a burial site, a yin abode, the most important factor is the site's ability to absorb "ti-chi," or earth energy.

A geomancer not only inspects the terrain surrounding a building, but must also consider the number of stories and rooms and the partitioning of the rooms. He must carefully survey all the doors in the building and distinguish them by size—large, medium, or small—and categorize them by type—ie. main doors, side doors, fire escapes, etc...

Generally, during a survey, the following factors are taken into consideration:

The "money-reserve spot" is located in the living room at the site accumulating, absorbing, and storing the most chi.

A bed should be positioned according to the location of doorways or openings that allow chi to enter and exit a room.

The orientation of the kitchen stove should be in accordance with the three auspicious orientations of the owner of the home.

A bathroom, preferably inconspicuous, should be located in unfavorable directions and balanced by potted plants.

Any well on the site should be located in a favorable direction.

Many geomancers have, however, neglected to consider the effects of the inflow and outflow of water into and away from a home. The entry and draining away of water from a house is quite important. In feng-shui, water is equivalent to money—fluid and always coursing. The movement of water generates a powerful influence upon its surroundings.

In my opinion, problems arising from the unfavorable flow of water are difficult to manage. It can be very hard for people living in such homes to avoid injury or death.

I had once inspected a home with a waterfall installed on the second story balcony. The waterfall was designed so that water pumped to the top of a pile of boulders cascaded down into a shallow pool. The owner was quite proud of the waterfall, which he himself had designed, so I felt reluctant to point out faults with the structure. After my departure, I informed his friend, the individual who had brought me to the house, of the problem.

"The rocks and waterfall are located at a spot correlating to the owner's neck. Please tell him to dismantle the waterfall, or some very serious disaster will result."

Despite the warning, the owner of this residence did not dismantle the waterfall. Three years later, he discovered a hard lump on his neck which medical tests revealed to be a malignant growth. The tumor on his neck in many ways resembled the rocks and waterfall in his home. He died soon after. At the time, this individual was the president of several factories and owner of a large restaurant. Young and already successful, he had a highly promising business career ahead. After receiving his diagnosis, he had come to see me. I gave him my blessings but shook my head, knowing it was too late for anything to be done.

In large buildings, water is often present in the decorative form of water fountains. When designed by expert geomancers to produce a calming, pleasing atmosphere, the introduction of water can increase customers and business.

In ordinary households, however, it is almost always inauspicious to dig pools or install fountains or waterfalls inside the home. If done merely for personal pleasure, such undertakings are unnecessary. There is usually no place inside a house favorable for such an extravagant introduction of water.

Ponds, swimming pools, and fountains built outside the home are acceptable. However, to ensure that such projects are installed in favorable positions—the northeast and southwest positions should be avoided for example—consult an expert geomancer.

There are two principles guiding the inflow and outflow of water:

1) Water entering the home should be noticeable, and water exiting the home should be hidden. Stated another way, water should flow in via overt ditches and flow out via covert ditches.

2) Water flowing toward the home should be a direct, straight stream. Water draining away should flow out by a winding, indirect channel.

These two principles concern the "harnessing" of wealth. A direct inflow of money with slow, indirect expenditures results in savings and abundance.

In the past, I, Living Buddha Lian-sheng, surveyed the feng-shui of a factory that conducted big business and had a huge gross income. Its expenditures, however, were astonishing. Despite the direct inflow of water chi at the front the building, there was a large drainage ditch behind the building that was too straight and exposed. To rectify the situation, I recommended the building of a bridge above the ditch. Such a bridge serves three functions:

1) compensation for the over-exposure of the ditch
2) the slowing and "locking in" of flowing water
3) improvement of foot traffic in the area.

The proper analysis of inflow and outflow of water requires a great deal of training and study.

25. The Importance of Workshops

In the United States, many households have workshops, often in their garages. Inside the garage, beside parked cars, various tools and equipment are stored. Since paying others to perform repair jobs can be costly, homeowners themselves often carry out ordinary repairs such as car tune-ups, water and electricity repairs, lawn mowing, and house painting. Even furniture purchased from stores often comes unassembled, and one must read the instructions to assemble the parts.

Because the workshop is an "activity room" with frequent movement, hammering, knocking, and other loud noises, its location inside a home greatly influences household feng-shui. Workshops are therefore very important.

Houses with basements may install workshops on this lower level. It is best if the basement is located either at the northwest position or at the lower, rear end of the dragon side of the house. By nature, workshops are often relatively untidy places and should not be located at the upper, front part of homes. The most appropriate design is to locate them below or behind at the northwest position.

Because garages commonly double as workshops, it is ideal

for a garage to be located at the northwest position in a home. A garage located at either the northeast or southwest position is unfavorable as workshops located in these positions can cause accidents, hindrances in work, and even family discord.

In the United States, some houses have adjoining garages detached from the main residence. Such garages should not be located at the front of the tiger side of the home. In such a position, the garage door opening becomes a "tiger's mouth," and a tiger's mouth that is too tall or too long may incur unfavorable accidents.

An adjoining garage should also not protrude too conspicuously. If such a protrusion already exists, it is preferable for the garage to be located on a slightly lower area on the tiger side in a position that does not overpower the dragon side. In America, almost every home has a garage, so the garage plays a very important role in household feng-shui, serving not only as a car park but also a workshop.

In Taiwan, the homes of the wealthy are not often equipped with garages. Occasionally simple sheds are built to house the cars. I would like to note here that special attention should be paid to the placement of the shed and its location on either the dragon side or tiger side of the home. Incorrect placements create unavoidable disasters of a great magnitude.

A car shed beside a home is the equivalent of a protruding object.

In the past, I had conducted many feng-shui readings for factory owners. The location of a household workshop is equivalent to the location and proper operation of machinery inside a factory. Properly installed machinery will run smoothly, but improperly installed machines may break down for no apparent reason. The quality of the machinery and its operation determines the quality of the product.

On one occasion, I had been asked to a factory to inspect

a huge machine that constantly broke down. The machine's frequent need for repairs gave factory workers numerous headaches, and even a technician, specially contracted from abroad, could not solve the problem. I was finally invited to take a look at the machine. I brought with me a bag of salt, a bag of rice, and a talisman inscribed with the words "continuous operation." After inspection, I saw that the machine had been incorrectly positioned directly above the teeth of the tiger's mouth. "The machine is being stopped by the tiger's teeth and cannot turn. It is best to move it to a different spot."

"But this is such a gigantic machine that the building housing it had been originally designed around it. To move it would be too expensive. Is there any other solution?" the owner pleaded with me.

Finally, I decided to resort to a "spiritual remedy." I performed a ritual and sprinkled salt and rice on the machine on a "Ch'u" date picked from the lunar calendar. I then pasted the talisman for "continuous operation" on the machine.

Strangely, the day after the ritual and pasting of the magic talisman, the machine began to operate smoothly. Once it started moving, it did not break down again. The entire factory staff broke into thunderous cheers, and the foreign technician shook his head, puzzled.

Someone approached me and asked, "How did you make the machine run?"

"I sprinkled some salt and rice on the tiger's mouth, and when the tiger shut its jaws, it spat out the machine. It was just as simple as that!" I laughed.

It is important to remember that workshops, garages, and machine rooms are rooms of "movement" that can alter feng-shui and create unusual phenomena. A geomancer must not overlook these three important sites as neglect of one area may result in a failure in the larger design.

26. Remedies for A Haunted House

Recently, True Buddha School students in Canada desired to establish a local chapter of our school in Queens Park, Vancouver. The house they planned to purchase there had a market value of two hundred thousand U.S. dollars. However, because the house was rumored to be haunted, there were no buyers and, at the time, the going rate was only one hundred thousand U.S. dollars.

The previous owner, a medical doctor, had hung himself inside the home. After his suicide, the house had been rented to two Native Americans who stayed momentarily but quickly moved away. They claimed they often found themselves being pushed off the bed at night, and on several occasions, awoke to find themselves on the front lawn outside the home. Inside the house, an endless stream of unusual phenomena—strange fires, odors, sounds, and sightings of ghost shadows—occurred daily.

The students in Canada then came to ask me if they should purchase the house.

"Yes," I replied. "Buy the house and let me take care of the problem. I will go and sleep in the house first."

In the majority of cases, haunted houses have disordered magnetic energy fields. What had disturbed the magnetic energy field of this particular house? The individual who had hung himself continued to grasp onto a strong hatred, and it was this hatred that threw the house's magnetic energy field into chaos.

In other cases, where nobody has died in a house, the problem can be attributed to the building materials. For example, beams used in the construction of a house originating from an old temple with attached spiritual energy may also cause the magnetic energy field to become disordered.

Still, in other cases, houses may become haunted by natural causes. Houses standing upon land with inherently chaotic magnetic energy fields have a high potential of becoming haunted. At such sites, a geomancer will find the needle of his geomantic compass vacillating continually from left to right and up and down. People living in such houses will be affected by haunting spirits. They will have unstable temperaments, meet with unexpected disasters, develop sudden terminal illnesses, and their children's personalities will rapidly deteriorate. Inhabitants will also be afflicted with neurosis and depression.

If a high degree of disorder exists in the magnetic energy field, spirits can direct their hatred and grievances towards occupants of the house. Foreign objects can actually materialize, objects can fly around, and strange sounds and shadows may play tricks on people.

Despite these obstacles, I encouraged my students to buy the haunted house. I knew that an understanding of the causes behind the chaotic magnetic energy field would allow us to better manage the problem. We only needed to eliminate the "undesirable factors."

After they purchase the house, I will employ the following two methods to rectify the situation:

1) After arriving at the haunted house, I will first locate the object in which the deceased doctor's spirit has taken up lodging. It may be the beam with which he hung himself, an image of a person or animal in the living room, a desk, a chair, or even a rock in the yard. After locating this object, I simply need to remove it from the house.

After removing the object with the attached spirit, I will perform a ritual to purify and establish a "boundary" around the house. I will use a Tantric Buddhist "boundary setting" method and invoke the Four Deva Kings and other devas to guard the house.

The removal of this noxious factor should then normalize the magnetic earth energy of the home so that it will no longer be haunted.

2) Upon arrival at the haunted house, I will call the doctor's spirit to come forth and explain to him that the house now has a new owner. I will also explain to him the workings of karma that will, hopefully, ameliorate his hatred. (Generally, however, ghosts who have committed suicide are filled with such strong hatred and resentment that they do not easily let go of their emotional attachments.)

I will tell him that this house is to be converted into a local chapter of the True Buddha School and that a plaque will be installed for him at the left side of the shrine. By making offerings to this spirit every morning and evening, it is our wish that his anger and hatred will be relinquished. It would be nice if he took up an interest in Buddhism as well. What spirit would not prefer accepting and enjoying offerings from humans to scaring them with mischievous activities?

I will likely try the second method first and, if it does not work, I will resort to the first. If the object to which the spirit is attached is a supporting beam, for example, it will be quite difficult to remove. If the spirit's anger will not be appeased, I may only be able to employ a "Ferocious Vajra Deity" method to evict the spirit. I will then follow this with a "suppression method" to prevent the beam from becoming repossessed. Finally, I will perform rituals to purify the house and establish a protective boundary around it.

"Living Buddha Lian-sheng, are you not afraid of ghosts?" one student asked.

"A hanging ghost can be terrifying, but I don't mind."

"Why not?"

"A person of 'upright chi' is fearless."

"Are haunted houses affected by feng-shui?"

"Yes. A ghost's hatred and resentment disturbs the magnetic energy field of a house."

When searching for a home, always try your best to learn about the previous owners to avoid the purchase of a haunted house. If you have already purchased a haunted house and are unable to rectify the situation, then you can come and find me, Living Buddha Lian-sheng!

27. Houses that Produce High-ranking Officials

The Secrets of Earth Magic has illuminated for me many secrets behind the inspection and reading of house designs.

Someone once asked me, "To become a high-ranking official, what kind of house should one live in?"

I answered, "One should live in houses characterized by 'three tiers of golden boughs and jade leaves, red snakes swirling around a seal, dragon buildings and phoenix pavilions, or powerful horned objects'."

"These terms are too profound and mysterious. Can you explain them in modern terms?" he asked.

Following are the explanations of these special terms:

1) Three tiers of golden boughs and jade leaves — The house lived in should be surrounded by three rows of houses—one to the right, one to the left, and one behind the home. These three tiers should all display the pattern known as "golden boughs and jade leaves." (Note: "three tiers" does not refer to three-story houses.)

On hilly terrain, one must note the topography and structures to the left, right, and back of the home to see if a "cradling pattern" gives rise to the three tiers.

2) Red snakes swirling around a seal — An analogy can be drawn between the location of a "master site" in a metropolitan area and the pinpointing of the center of a fingerprint. By tracing patterns of swirling earth energy, one can locate this central point, "the seal amidst a swirl of red snakes." Such a site, however, takes an expert geomancer to locate.

The house of Yasuhiro Nakasone, the former Japanese prime minister, fits this description of "red snakes swirling around a seal."

3) Dragon buildings and phoenix pavilions — The terms "dragon" and "phoenix" characterize outstanding and distinguished personalities. A grand home resembling a spiraling dragon or soaring phoenix fits this description. Again, only expert geomancers can detect such designs.

4) Powerful horned objects — Inside a small and shabby residence, an expert geomancer can install "powerful horn-like objects" to bring fame, success, and prestige to people living within the home. If installed properly, such objects can lead one to become a high-ranking official. Improper installation, however, can bring multiple misfortunes.

To properly conduct these readings, geomancers first must learn to classify landforms and surrounding structures according to the five elements. They should then be able to interpret special formations using the generative and destructive relationships among the five elements. The following verses from *The Secrets of Earth Magic* present some of these relationships:

Earth's Imperial Edict has a Wooden Seal
Fire's Imperial Edict has a Metal Seal
Metal's Imperial Edict has a Wooden Seal
Water's Imperial Edict comes from the North
Wood's Imperial Edict comes from the South

Information from a site that generates a high official allows one to predict the ranking such an official will achieve and the duration of this official's stay in power.

In general, individuals with military careers should live in pointed houses, as "sharp" designs indicate power. To the right and left of these homes, there should also be the presence of "Guardians of Virtue," pointed formations providing the home with nourishing energy. A flawed, protruding shape, however, may turn a "general's home" into a home that produces pawns or powerful scoundrels.

Although the following quote refers to burial site feng-shui, it can also be applied to residential homes:

A military official emerges when "Guardians of Virtue" shine,

A "Craving Wolf" with a flat-top is matched by the "Fire Star;"

Cradled by drum and flag, facing a knife-shaped desk, One rises swiftly to seize military power.

Although burial sites thrive primarily on earth chi and residential homes on vital chi, these two forms of chi accompany one another and follow the same principles. Water flowing across land, for example, follows a course shaped by the topography of the land, and vapor above the water also moves along to the same course. Both water and vapor follow the same path.

The principles concerning houses that produce high-ranking officials are highly secret, and these teachings are rarely transmitted to people. Such information is truly invaluable. Without the special knowledge of feng-shui experts, however, interpreting such sites is a difficult task.

Among my students, there is one whose son, from my observations, bears the facial signs associated with the making of a high-ranking official. I instructed this student to install a "powerful object" in his small house. His son is currently the top student in his class and, in the future, will earn a doctorate degree. Eventually, through his involvement in politics, he will rise to a top-ranking government position.

An honest official with great writing talent,
A judge bearing the imperial seal,
A true scholar from dragon and phoenix abodes,
The hall of fame will sing his praises.

My knowledge and experiences in residential feng-shui can create powerful transformations. Utilizing a home's vital chi, an impoverished young man shall rise and transform into a high-ranking political figure.

28. Houses that Produce Wealth

I once performed a feng-shui reading for a man living inside a dilapidated house built of blocks of hardened earth. This house was located inside a bamboo grove. "The people living in this house will definitely become very rich," I told the owner.

Skeptically he replied, "My grandfather lived in this house and died of starvation. My father lived in this house and was stricken with poverty and illness. I am now living here and have not yet accomplished much with my life. Your words are quite hard to believe."

"The time has not yet come, but soon, you will definitely become wealthy," I replied.

"What is the basis for your prediction?" he asked.

"The front door of your house faces the flow of a watercourse which flows from the northeast direction. This fits the feng-shui pattern known as 'ken mountain and ken water paying homage to ants and wasps.' You will definitely accumulate great wealth."

"Is there anything else?"

"Your house is built of earthen blocks and sits upon land of the fire element. As fire generates earth, this indicates that days of prosperity are near."

"Why was my family not prosperous before? Why must we wait till later?"

I quoted him the following verse:

Inner arms are turning away,
Outer arms look back.
Distant peaks also return to keep guard.
Distant protection indicates initial poverty,
Followed by later prosperity.

Soon after my feng-shui reading, a construction company took interest in a plot of land on the hillside owned by this owner. With the builder supplying the finances and the owner supplying the land, the dry field was transformed into a residential subdivision of "country style villas." Surprisingly, all the houses were immediately sold the instant they were offered on the market.

The owner of the earthen house made a large sum of money from that deal. With that money, he purchased more land and built more houses. Successive projects flourished, and the owner himself eventually became the president of a large construction company. He is currently a very wealthy man with large holdings in real estate. He rides in luxurious cars, smokes the best cigars, and dresses in elegant suits.

Yet every night before retiring, his chauffeur secretly drives him back to his dilapidated house in the bamboo grove to sleep. With the exception of minor interior improvements, he did not dare alter anything in his earthen house. He firmly believes that this house has brought him his wealth and prosperity.

Why was the prosperity preceded by initial impoverishment?

Inner arms turning away — Instead of cradling the house, landforms to the right and left of the house are turned away at an angle indicating initial poverty.

Outer arms looking back — Looking out the front door, mountainous landforms in the distance to the left and right, however, turn back to look after the house indicating future prosperity.

Distant peaks returning to keep guard — The mountain peaks in the far distance are turned around to look after and protect the house.

This feng-shui arrangement allowed me to boldly make my predictions.

In formulating my analysis, I also take the five elements into consideration. I first determine the guardian element of the owner, as each individual is born under the guardianship of one of the five elements of metal, wood, water, fire, or earth. The land on which the house sits is then also classified as metal, wood, water, fire, or earth. With knowledge of the nourishing and destructive cycles of the five elements, one can evaluate the combined effects of the elements and discern whether or not they indicate prosperity.

Also, as soon as I enter a house, I locate the "money-reserve spot." I employ special methods to enhance the money-reserve spot's ability to gather chi and wealth.

Here is a verse on "how to get rich":

Prosperous chi entering the living room,
Fills the treasuries.
Remember to keep the evergreens green,
And the household will certainly bloom and blossom.

A good pattern is for a residential home to be built with its back facing the northeast (ken) direction. From the house, one should see water coming from the southwest (shen) direction. Living under such circumstances, one will become rich so rapidly that one's treasury will quickly fill with gold and silver. There will be such great wealth knocking at one's door that one will not be able to turn it away even if one wanted to.

The formulas for locating houses that produce great wealth cannot be bought with money. The mere ability to determine whether a house is auspicious is not enough; geomancers who cannot also help owners generate great wealth and fortune are not true professionals.

I know from my many years of study and practice in the art of geomancy that feng-shui is a very profound subject. It is unfortunate that many are easily taken in by eloquent feng-shui practitioners who are without much efficacy. Such practitioners have, indeed, discredited the art of geomancy.

The secret formulas to houses producing great wealth are indeed priceless!

29. Fear of Dying at Twenty-Eight

In a feng-shui reading I once came across a unique and very strange case.

The family to which I am referring lived in an old compound with houses surrounding a central courtyard. Two branches of this family's clan had experienced quite inexplicable tragedies: all the males had died at the age of twenty-eight.

The father died of an illness at twenty-eight. An uncle's whereabouts overseas became unknown the year he turned twenty-eight. The eldest son, at age twenty-eight, fell to his death while climbing a mountain. The second son died of cancer at twenty-eight.

Now the third son was fast approaching twenty-eight. His fear of dying an early death led him to many temples to pray and seek consultations. The answers he received, however, were all different and made him very anxious.

The family was very large and several members invited me to inspect their ancestors' burial sites as well as their living quarters in hopes of ascertaining the cause of this curse which resulted in death at twenty-eight.

My inspection revealed nothing wrong with their ancestors' burial sites, however, there were several shortcomings in the design of their living quarters. I pointed out the various flaws and suggested they quickly remedy the situations.

The family compound was built amidst a grove of trees in the countryside. Many ponds surrounded the compound—some with water, some dry, and some almost dry. Upon examining the ponds more closely, I found many problems. Water from one pond entered the courtyard of the compound, while water from another pond pointed at two houses on the side. One pond even had its water pointing at the main door.

First I told the family to fill the dry ponds. I then asked them to modify the ponds that had water into crescent shapes with the inner curves facing the compound (so the compound would be "inside the bows").

The front quarter of this quadrangle compound was very tall, but the newer quarter at the back of the compound, which was built after the first, was too low in comparison. Such cases, where the front of a house is taller than the rear, indicate a loss of members, particularly young family members.

I asked the family to remodel the rear quarter of the compound and bring it to the same height as the front quarter. I told them it was very important that houses at the back be at the same height as houses at the front.

They followed my recommendations and made the changes.

They then asked, "Why did the men all die at the age of twenty-eight?"

Offhand, it was quite difficult for me to explain. I replied, "There must be a connection somewhere in this compound with the number twenty-eight. For example, when you add them up, there may be a total of twenty-eight pillars or a total of twenty-eight trees surrounding this compound. Or there may be twenty eight stoves, twenty-eight beams, or twenty-eight doors...."

"Twenty-eight stoves? We cannot possibly have that many stoves!" they exclaimed.

"I don't think so either," I said with a smile. "That was just an example."

Later, they told me they indeed counted and found a total of twenty-eight supporting pillars around the compound. They were impressed with the prediction.

They asked, "Does this mean we should add more pillars?"

"No," I replied. "Do you think increasing the number of pillars to one hundred will allow everyone to live to be one hundred years old? The number of pillars was just one factor in determining the age of death. The main causes lay in the ponds and the fact that the front of the compound was taller than the rear."

I explained, "Too little pond water indicated an inability to live to a full age. The corners of the ponds pointing directly at the main door and the side houses fit the feng-shui pattern known as 'penetrating the heart and shooting the cheeks.' It signified the inauspicious phenomenon of male members dying young.

"The heights of the front and rear houses represented the different generations in the family. The front houses represent former generations and the rear houses represent later generations. The low height of the rear houses indicated a loss of younger members of the family. It is proper for the rear part of a house to be at the same level or taller than the front part of a house. A lower rear house signifies great disaster."

Ten years after inspecting this large quadrangle compound, the family told me that, after making the modifications, people living in the compound have enjoyed greater peace. Several male members have lived past twenty-eight without encountering serious catastrophes. Their fears of dying at twenty-eight have now been dispelled.

I, Living Buddha Lian-sheng, am particularly good at identifying houses that can cause "undue deaths in the family." I also can identify houses that "bear no children."

In *The Secrets of Earth Magic*, there is the following verse:
Without protrusion, members will be scarce,
Without earth chi, no child will be born;
With high pressure, all children die,
With assault from water, no child can survive.

A house completely devoid of protrusions is inauspicious for it signifies a lonely household with few members. If the topography of the land is so flat that there is little presence of earth chi, the household will not have any children. Great overbearing forces oppressing the house from all sides also can cause miscarriages and the breaking off of a bloodline. In cases where water directly points at a house on all four sides, not even a single child will remain!

A house located before or behind a temple may also exhibit the above phenomena because its earth chi is already drawn up by the temple.

The presence or absence of earth chi has a great impact on the feng-shui of a house. In truth, only a geomancer with the ability to read earth chi can be considered a true expert. The earth chi of a house not only affects the number of people in a family but also impacts their health. As a final word of caution: do not live on land devoid of earth chi.

30. Peach Blossom Luck in Married Couples

As mentioned in a previous chapter, placement of the kitchen faucet (water) directly across from the stove (fire) is a feng-shui feature inviting "peach blossom luck."

If, beyond the front door, one has two different kinds of trees, one on the right and one on the left, this also invites "peach blossom luck."

A very steep slope directly behind the house and a pond shaped like a woman's eyebrow in front of the house signifies that males of the house will have "peach blossom luck." Such a feng-shui pattern indicates that, from generation to generation, fathers and sons will marry two wives.

Features that invite "peach blossom luck" for men include the following:

• Vines twining around a tree in front of the house — This indicates a "hard-to-shake" entanglement.

• Water from a metal-element mountain directly facing the front door — This indicates that males of the house are handsome, "lady's men."

• A mountain in front of the house resembling a desk that is toppled sideways as if dancing — This indicates that the man likes to loaf about.

Features that invite "peach blossom luck" for women include the following:

• A tree in front of the house that is swollen on both the top and the bottom — This indicates a propensity for promiscuity.

• A watercourse in front of the house that reverses its flowing direction — This indicates adultery.

• Two watercourses in front of the house, rapidly flowing away — This indicates elopement with another man.

• Beams of the house with floral designs carved upon them — This indicates that the woman will be obsessed with men.

• A forked road on the white tiger side of the house with the tiger side of the house directly facing the intersection of the fork's tines — This indicates the woman will have many men.

• A smaller convenience door beside the main door — This indicates the wanting of both parties.

I once performed a feng-shui reading for a family whose male members, from the great-grandfather's generation to the great-grandson's, all had two wives. It turned out that the slope behind the family house was very steep and there was an eyebrow shaped pond in front of the house. In addition, two different kinds of trees had been growing outside the front door.

In my feng-shui readings, I have also come across cases where forked roads are right beside the tiger side of homes. One must understand that forked roads are like beauties, exposing and offering themselves. A forked road next to the tiger side can have a powerful impact on women in the household. An innocent and pure woman may become loose and wanton.

Such developments are undesirable as they are destructive to normal family life. Peach blossom luck, whether inflicted upon a man or woman, is disastrous and invites instability. Only certain individuals can benefit somewhat from peach blossom luck—actors and actresses. A handsome actor or beautiful actress with peach blossom luck will attract many fans and be admired and loved by greater numbers of people. With such individuals, the greater the peach blossom luck, the greater their sex appeal and popularity.

Homes of the wealthy often have front doors so large they are difficult to open. For convenience sake, smaller side doors are occasionally added next to the front door. But, this gives a house two openings: it gives "convenience" to oneself but also to others. "Wanting both the big door and the small door" is a sign of disastrous peach blossom luck. It is acceptable to have a smaller door in addition to the main door as long as the smaller door is a sufficient distance from the latter. Avoid having the large and small doors right beside one another.

Geomancers know that "undesirable water courses ruining a prosperous spot" are waters associated with peach blossom luck. Men and women under the spells of such peach blossom luck are lost, trapped by desires, and unable to control their fanciful and fickle hearts. The presence of murmuring water or water running towards one's house with a sudden reversal and flowing away of water before the front of the door are undesirable feng-shui features associated with adulterous elopement.

The combination of water in front of the house and the presence of many secluded trees at the back of the house is a sign that the woman of the house may become involved in licentious and incestuous relationships.

To quote the feng-shui verse:
Water reversing its course leads to licentiousness,
A forked road appears as a naked display;
Even a chaste girl from a good family,
Will wind up in bed with two lovers.
An individual in a marriage stricken with peach blossom

luck is like a rock tossed into the quiet lake of family life. Ripples appear. If one does not make appropriate changes, divorce and family break up may result. Those who can tolerate infidelity will face the co-existence of wife and mistress. For those who cannot tolerate such situations, there are divorce courts.

The Secrets of Earth Magic advises that feng-shui features associated with the invitation of peach blossom luck be removed and avoided. Once peach blossom luck is stirred, it is not easily managed or kept under control.

I, Living Buddha Lian-sheng, have in my lifetime helped thousands of men and women solve problems of varying magnitudes caused by sexual indiscretions. Feng-shui treatments to correct undesirable features in their homes and Tantric methods of purification and subjugation have been employed. Some of the stories I have encountered are so intriguing I could write thousands and thousands of novels based on them.

In summary, whether brought upon a man or a woman, peach blossom luck is undesirable. It can bring a sudden turn of unforeseen events and turmoil to family life. If handled inappropriately, great resentment and even suicide may result.

31. Feng-shui Associated with Twins

Two students of mine, a husband and wife from Vancouver, Canada, came one day to see me. Chao Shao-tung and his wife, both young and intelligent, are currently the editors-in-chief of the monthly journal *True Buddha Bodhi*.

The young man Chao Shao-tung has delicate features and his wife is kind and gentle. The couple is a rare one in that both partners practice Buddhism. Both are also talented linguists who speak fluent English, Mandarin, and Cantonese.

They said to me, "Grand Master, we have a request to make."

"What is it?"

"We would like to have twins," they replied kneeling before me.

"Twins? Why?" I asked surprised.

"The study and practice of Buddhism is very important to us and life is so short. We would like to have two children, but with two separate births, it will take a lot of time to raise the children. If we could have twins, it will save us a lot of time, and we can devote more time to our practice. This is our wish, and we hope Grand Master can help us."

Upon hearing this, I could not help but smile. I replied, "I can give you a blessing and also pray to the Buddhas on your behalf. May you be granted twins." Chao Shao-tung and his wife are a very sincere and devoted couple of high moral character and rare talents. They will be future pillars of the True Buddha School!

This request for twins brought back memories of an interesting feng-shui case I once encountered in a small village in Kaohsiung. There, eight out of every ten families had twins!

At the time, the village council, the learned in the community, and the residents themselves were mystified. Why were so many families having twins?

I paid a visit to the village and discovered that the mysterious twin births had to do with the locale's feng-shui. From the main road at the village entrance, I saw two metal-element mountains located near one another, like two breasts or two bellies, one in front and one behind. Readings from my geomantic compass revealed a watercourse running from the "kuei" direction toward the twin mountains.

This feng-shui arrangement, twin mountains connected like breasts receiving water from the "kuei" direction, is a known pattern associated with the appearance of twins.

Another feng-shui feature associated with twins is a door of a main room directly facing a fire-element mountain and the entering of water in double channels around the house.

The Secrets of Earth Magic contains the following verse:
Why is there the prevalence of twin births?
Twin chi faces the main living room;
An examination of earth chi in surrounding mountains and waters
Allows one to make reasonable assertions with assurance.

Why then do families with twins also have single births?

This is a result of the "waxing and waning of chi." One may live at a location with feng-shui features for twin births, but the energy of the earth waxes and wanes. Conception during a time when "the twin births earth chi" is in a waning phase will result in a single birth.

The orientation of one's front door also plays a significant role. Whether the front door faces the twin mountains or fire-element mountain in a direct or oblique manner makes a difference. Such features account for twin births and single births, and these factors also explain the single births in the village of Kaohsiung where twin births predominated.

In general, feng-shui features of sites producing large families are as follows:

A metal-element landform is seen from the front. This landform is layered and contains positive, nourishing elements such as vibrant earth chi. Landforms protect and cradle the site on the dragon and tiger sides, and the front of the site is wide and spacious with no destructive features to the left or to the right.

Feng-shui features associated with few family members are as follows:

Land with flat topography lacking earth chi; a watercourse (wet or dry) running toward the front of the house; houses situated in front of or behind temples.

Additionally, the following feng-shui verse describes features associated with infertility (the trigrams in the verse refer to those in Later Heaven Circle):

High formation in sun,
Single peak at li and tui,
Blooming flowers and the presence of ponds in kun,
All may lead to infertility.

Feng-shui is an extremely intriguing subject. The more one studies it, the more fascinating one finds it to be.

32. The House of Endless Illnesses

I have found many problems with houses in the United States. Perhaps in building homes in forests and woods, Americans are responding to a natural instinct to live among nature. Even if they do not live in the woods, many live in homes surrounded by big trees. Often these trees are located directly outside the front door, behind the home, encircling and enshrouding the house.

When I first arrived in the United States, many of my American students invited me to inspect their homes when they learned that I performed feng-shui readings. As a result, I have studied quite a number of American homes. Though average Americans may appear tall and strong, they are no healthier than other races.

Moore, an American student of mine, said to me, "For the past three years, every member of my family has taken turns getting sick. As soon as one gets better, another becomes ill. There has been no break at all. We've spent vast sums of money on medical bills, yet the physical and mental suffering has been even worse."

He called his house "the house of endless illnesses."

The first thing I noticed upon visiting his home was a large tree with branches towering over the house. The house was not big, and the tree was huge in comparison. Luxuriant, well-spaced leaves completely covered the house. The trunk of the tree was huge, and roots extended beneath the home.

In such houses, residents have their yang-chi sucked away by the yin-chi of the large tree. With an excess of yin-chi over-powering the yang-chi, how can one avoid becoming sick?

I told Moore to move away as living in a house under such a large tree would definitely be detrimental to his family's health. The proper mix of yin and yang energies in a residential home is very important. As it would be too difficult to relocate the large tree, the best thing for him would be to move. After some convincing, Moore finally agreed.

Geomancers have pointed out various harmful situations that may lead to the breakout of numerous diseases and ailments. Occupants living in the following houses are vulnerable:

— A house with watercourses directed at it from the four directions of tzu, wu, yu, and mao (i.e., north, south, west, and east respectively.)

— A house with roads pointed at it from the four directions of tzu, wu, yu, and mao.

— A house covered up by a huge tree with roots extending beneath the house.

— Water from the ken (northeast) direction pointing at the front door.

— Large rocks or artificial boulders piled at the front door as landscape design.

— A house that is either too bright or too dim.

— A bathroom (toilet) connected with the kitchen, a manure pile next to a well, or a bathroom facing the front door.

— The improper placement of heavy objects.

— Too narrow of a distance between the front door and backyard, and a steep, imposing hill behind the house.

I once performed a feng-shui reading for an individual named Fable. As soon as I walked through his front door, I could touch the wall to the backyard. The house was long from right to left and its backyard was rocky and steep. I said to him, "You have some health problems."

"No," he replied. "I have always been pretty healthy."

It was true that Fable was tall and muscular with rosy cheeks. The people around us were surprised to hear me make that statement.

I said, "This is a minor illness, but the pain caused is unbearable."

"To what illness are you referring?"

"Hemorrhoids."

Fable's face turned a deep red and he said, "Grand Master, you are right. I indeed have had hemorrhoids for many years and the pain is quite unbearable at times. But how did you know?"

"When the distance between the front door and the back of the house is narrow, and the land behind the house is too steep and piled with hard rocks, one will have hemorrhoids."

"What about apartment houses with no hills or rocky slopes? How are readings done then?"

"An apartment house may not have hills or rocky slopes, but 'pressing and narrow' features can still exist. According to feng-shui theories, pressing conditions have the same impact as steep conditions, and narrow features are similar to 'hard' features," I explained.

The Secrets of Earth Magic states:
In the presence of —
  — The Luo-ho and Ji-do Stars, the chest suffers;
  — Swallow's nest on a beam, recalcitrant skin sores grow;
  — A manure pit facing the front door, the belly is bloated;
  — A hollow on the oncoming dragon, insanity develops;

— *Chaotic rocks near the mouth of a well, limbs are broken;*
— *Worn out doors and pillars, multiple sores grow.*

33. The Formation of Haunted Houses

The following is a verse from *The Secrets of Earth Magic*:
A front door at the northeast position allows ghosts to enter;
Because not one of the three yangs shine upon that spot,
Through portals of extreme yin,
Ghosts enter and converge.
Making noises in walls and all sorts of disturbances,
They causing mischief in dark places,
Hiding among the banana leaves.

The ken (northeast) position on a geomantic compass is associated with the presence of ghosts. A front door installed at the northeast position is known as a "ghost door" in feng-shui. It is a spot of "extreme yin," "not shone upon by the three kinds of yang." Most ghosts will enter houses with ghost doors and hide themselves in dim and dark places, dark bedrooms, or areas with potted plants.

Though one may have positioned one's bed correctly inside the bedroom, fitful sleep and dreams of demons and monsters may still plague. The presence of ghosts converging to steal one's chi can leave one in a state of complete exhaustion.

If a door is a northeast door and one becomes pregnant, it is possible that one will have an unusual pregnancy or a strange looking baby. There will be odd signs during the pregnancy, and the child may be mute or deaf. In some cases, one may think one is pregnant, but instead, find a tumor or cyst in the belly.

In the past I had inspected the feng-shui of a house that was haunted.

The owner asked me, "Why is my house haunted?"

I replied, "The front door is at the northeast ghost door position."

"But everything was fine at the beginning when we first moved in," the owner retorted.

"There must have been a death in the family which then led the ghosts to come in."

"When did this happen?"

"Two years ago."

At this point, the owner nodded and agreed with me. Two years ago, his mother died, and funeral services were performed for three months in the home. Ever since, family members had been afflicted with endless nightmares and strange things often occurred inside the house. His wife had an operation to remove a uterine fibroid tumor and had been sick ever since. There was much unrest in the household.

I instructed the owner to remove the northeast ghost door.

The situation could have been more serious if, in addition to having a northeast door, the house had been a large mansion without much sunlight shining upon it. It might have even turned into a ghost market with ghosts converging to do business. Then it would truly have been a wonder if people could live in such houses peacefully.

In addition to a northeast ghost door, one should also pay attention to the following factors that may turn a house into a home for ghosts and demons:

— Any damage to the walls of the house should be promptly repaired.

— Corridors should be connected to living areas. Do not leave any space between the two.

— An open space must not take the shape of a coffin.

— Pay attention to small sheds behind the house to ensure that they do not look like coffins.

— Avoid placing houseplants in spots high in yin chi.

Negligence in the above areas may invite ghosts to gather.

Why should one quickly repair damage to the walls of a house? Ghosts are fond of houses with ruined walls because coffins are stored in similar sites. To ghosts, coffin-shaped open areas and spaces between corridors and living areas are often mistaken for coffins. The same reasoning applies to a small shed built behind the main house. Such small sheds will appear to be coffins to the ghosts. Potted plants in places with an accumulation of yin chi also invite a convergence of ghosts.

I, Living Buddha Lian-sheng, have encountered numerous ghosts in my life. By nature, ghosts are mischievous, but they are also straightforward and simple. I am not afraid of them. In fact, I am more afraid of human beings than ghosts. Many humans are manipulative and deceptive and more frightening than any ghost.

As a Tantrayana practitioner, I know how to perform "food offerings," "transformation of nectar" rituals, and "soul deliverances." I make it a habit to perform these three rituals every other day at home. Because of this, many ghosts also converge at my house! They come not because there are features that give rise to haunted houses, but rather because I summon them to come. I am sympathetic to them and perform deliverance rituals to help them. Ghosts are also sentient beings.

I have been performing these rituals solely out of compassion, expecting nothing in return. After all, attaining rebirth into this world is not always an easy task, and if I can do something to benefit others, it is my wish to do as much as I can.

PART II

34. Reflections on Writing this Book

I, Living Buddha Lian-sheng, was originally a Christian. I then became a student of Taoism and studied feng-shui under Taoist Master Ch'ing Chen. Eventually I took refuge in Buddhism, first in the exoteric schools and later in the esoteric (Tantric) schools.

When I met Taoist Master Ch'ing Chen in Taiwan, he had renounced secular life and was living anonymously as a hermit. Although a Taoist of the Ch'ing Cheng School, his knowledge was not confined to Taoism; he also had a profound understanding of the theories and practices of both Sutric and Tantric Buddhism. In fact, a closer look at the Master's lineage will reveal Vajra Master Jung Tseng and Vajra Master Norras to be his fellow disciples.

Taoist Master Ch'ing Chen was a scholar and expert in many arts and disciplines. His interests covered a vast array of subjects, and among his extensive book collections were priceless secret teachings that have never circulated publicly.

In his later years, Taoist Master Ch'ing Chen devoted himself to the mystical practices of t'u-na (breathing) and the tempering of the spirit. After attaining freedom and a complete mastery of the self, he preferred not to bring up any of the miraculous deeds he had performed while living in mainland China. I was his only student and he had taught me Taoism, Sutric Buddhism, Tantric Buddhism, and feng-shui. His unsurpassed feng-shui knowledge was an invaluable treasure, and I feel extremely fortunate to have studied and learned from him.

From all my years of studying and practicing Taoism, exoteric Buddhism, esoteric Buddhism, and feng-shui, I have learned many secrets between Heaven and Earth. I would like to follow in the footsteps of my master, living a life of seclusion. However, I now have many students of my own who continually seek me out to record my feng-shui knowledge. It seems that the more I run from fame, the more fame seeks me out; the harder I try to live in seclusion, the more I am sought out. This is an embarrassing and painful situation for me.

Since becoming a monk, I have realized the pathway that can transform and expand an ordinary existence into a transcendent one. I have also understood the principles and method for immortality. With the mind and consciousness in accord with the Buddhas, I have attained realization and awakened to the true nature of the Mind. I had no longer intended to write any more articles about feng-shui. But I was approached by men of great virtue, here and overseas, who, knowing that I had studied the secrets of feng-shui, urged me to write a book detailing the practice of household feng-shui. They reasoned that if I kept this treasure hidden in my bosom, one day this treasure would disappear from the world.

Therefore, writing *Household Feng-shui* after becoming a monk was also a surprise to myself.

The writing of this book has been quite a difficult task as the field of feng-shui is replete with special terms. If my writing had been too obscure, no student or reader would understand it. Therefore, for beginners, I have refrained from using too many specialized feng-shui terms and have avoided writing anything too deep.

My foremost wish in writing *Household Feng-shui* is to make this book accessible to all readers. I have tried to present the details incisively and inspiringly so the reader will not feel bogged down by the material.

Of course, this book serves only as a basic introduction to *The Secrets of Earth Magic*, as the former covers only one thousandth of the latter's content. *The Secrets of Earth Magic* is divided into twelve sections, comprising of a total of seventy-two chapters. In this latest writing, I have only selected the important points from several chapters. Most of this book is, in fact, based on my own encounters and experiences from putting my feng-shui knowledge into practice.

I know in my heart that the information in this book is valid. I have inspected thousands of houses and proof that this feng-shui knowledge works far exceeds the successes cited in this book. There are numerous feng-shui methods of analyzing residential abodes or burial sites. Initially, these methods may appear easy to learn, but they are actually hard to master. And though the breadth of this book is only a tiny fraction of feng-shui knowledge, the study of this tiny fraction may take one's entire life.

Many household feng-shui books (written in Chinese) on the market today employ methods of "directions" and are written in such obscure language that one cannot bear to read them. Some of the "fashionable masters" use tricks to cheat people. I have therefore decided to write this book using reason and logic, eliminating the usual mystique that shrouds the subject.

In regard to the feng-shui theories pertaining to "Three Harmonies," "Three Eras," "Nine Palaces," "Nine Stars," "Five

139

Elements," "Twenty-eight Constellations," "Mysterious Void," "Eight Trigrams," and "Twenty-four Mountains," I hope that, in the future, there will be a chance for me to offer classes on these topics in a systematic way. I have been invited to teach a feng-shui class at the University of Washington and, if this does materialize, I believe it will be enjoyed by both Chinese and American students.

I realize that only by teaching everything in a systematic, prescribed order can students learn and progress gradually from the easiest feng-shui concepts to the most difficult. I am carefully considering the possibility of offering a class on *The Secrets of Earth Magic.*

Earth energy also plays a role in transcending "worldly practices." In spiritual cultivation, the cultivator seeks to maneuver his own vital energy, integrating it with the vital energy of Heaven and Earth. That is the reason behind a Tantric practitioner's search for caves of high energy to retreat to. Maneuvering one's vital energy to join the vital energy of Heaven and Earth is a requisite to Merging and Union.

The ultimate attainment in Tantrayana practice is the precise maneuvering of one's internal energy to identify and merge with the energy of Heaven and Earth, and to then transmute this energy into Emptiness.

Knowledge of geomancy averts future perils.
A practitioner obtains long-lasting peace,
A gold-filled treasury,
As well as benefits in spiritual cultivation.
This all-encompassing knowledge
Brings goodness and many benefits to the world.

35. A Sign of Affirmation from Heaven for the True Buddha School

The following is an account of the Blessing Ceremony held at the Ling Shen Ching Tze Temple in Redmond, Washington, USA in February, 1987.

On February 7th, 1987, the True Buddha School held its annual lunar New Year Blessing Ceremony at the Ling Shen Ching Tze Temple in Redmond, Washington. About one thousand students from around the world attended the ceremony.

Masters attending the ceremony included: John Chen, Chen Sen-ho, Chen Sen-lung, Chung Lu-sheng, Li Mei-li, Li Hsing-chih, Lu Li-hsiang, Luo Chen-fang, Kender Tomko, and Cheng Yu-hsin—from the United States; Liao Yun-ling, Lai Wen-yan—from Canada; Liu Yi-jung—from Hong Kong; Yu Yin-shou, Chuang Huang-yu, and Liao Yu-tsun—from Taiwan.

Three Tibetan lamas were present: Budon Chinchu, Tsangdui Gyalpo, and Sonje Gyaltso. They all offered katas to Living Buddha Lian-sheng and received blessings from the Living Buddha in return. Rev. Wu-beng, a Buddhist monk from an exoteric school, took refuge in Living Buddha Lian-sheng at the ceremony.

Liu Yi-li and a group of True Buddha School students from Vancouver, Canada were on their way to the ceremony at the Redmond temple when Liu suddenly noticed an extraordinary phenomenon in the sky directly above the Ling Shen Ching Tze Temple. A beam of brilliant, milky white light was descending from the sky and pouring into the temple. To the side, another beam of brilliant green light was also descending from the sky and pouring into another side of the temple. At their interface, the two beams of brilliant light merged, forming a spectacular sight. Pulling their car off the road, the students all got out to take a look at this phenomenal sight.

On the evening of February 8th, Liu Yi-li stood up and told everyone of the miraculous sight she had witnessed. The descending and merging of the two lights was an empowerment for all of the sentient beings present.

At 10:00 a.m. on February 7th, the Blessing Ceremony began. As the assembly stood with great respect, bells and gongs sounded in welcome during the ceremonial entrance of the founder of the True Buddha School, the Holy Red Crown Vajra Master Living Buddha Lian-sheng. The founder gave the following verses to commemorate the occasion:

Happiness resides in one's mind,
The mind is the Buddha;
Once the mind harbors the Buddha,
Happiness naturally follows.

After the burning of the ceremonial prayer pamphlet, Living Buddha Lian-sheng proceeded in accordance with the Blessing Ceremony liturgy—first the purification mantras, then the invocation mantras, great homage, offering, fourfold refuge, armor protection, sutra chanting, dance of mudras, visualization, mantra chanting, entering into samadhi, and finally the blessing empowerment. During the ceremony, a strong spiritual energy pervaded the entire temple. Dharma rain showered and Buddha light shone upon everyone in the assembly. All present received great blessings from the Buddhas.

Living Buddha Lian-sheng noted in the ceremonial prayer that all who had registered for the ceremony by mail would also receive great blessings from the Dakinis. The registration forms were burnt along with the ceremonial prayer.

For two afternoons, the masters took turns giving teachings to the students at the temple.

On February 7th, at 8:00 p.m., Living Buddha Lian-sheng gave a discourse on "The Boundless Mind"and the "Four Immeasurable Minds."

May all beings have happiness and the causes of happiness — this is immeasurable loving-kindness.

May all beings be liberated from suffering and the causes of suffering — this is immeasurable compassion.

May all beings be free from suffering and always stay happy — this is immeasurable joy.

May all beings be free from grasping and aversion toward others, and develop faith in the equality of all — this is immeasurable equanimity.

Loving-kindness, compassion, joy, and equanimity are the Four Immeasurable Minds. After explaining the steps of the practice and the secret method to engender these four immeasurable minds, Living Buddha Lian-sheng gave the empowerment to all students present.

The teaching of the Four Immeasurable Minds affirmed the great white light above the Ling Shen Ching Tze Temple as the "light of loving-kindness and compassion."

On February 8th, at 8:00 p.m., Living Buddha Lian-sheng gave a discourse on the visualization of Manjushri Bodhisattva's Sword Practice. After sharing the secrets of this practice with the assembly, Living Buddha Lian-sheng also gave the empowerment for this practice.

While the Living Buddha was explaining the visualization for the Manjushri practice, red and yellow blossoms fell from the spiritual realm and a great spiritual energy filled the auditorium. Many students moved their hands spontaneously to form the Lotus Holding Mudra. It was a wonderful moment. Many students themselves saw the showering of red and yellow blossoms from above.

Living Buddha Lian-sheng announced, "With the showering of flowers upon the assembly, everyone will receive auspiciousness and their disasters will be removed. Manjushri Bodhisattva is the Auspiciousness Vajra as well as the Prajna (Wisdom) Vajra."

The teaching of the Manjushri Sword Visualization affirmed the great green light above the Ling Shen Ching Tze Temple as the "light of wisdom."

The Living Buddha stated, "Wisdom and Compassion are the two requisite qualities spiritual cultivators must have before they can help lead sentient beings to liberation. Wisdom without loving-kindness and compassion will eventually turn one into a demon. Compassion without wisdom will only help a limited number of sentient beings. To yield the greatest power, there must be a union of these two lights."

The following projects proposed by students deserve special mention:

Chung Hsiao-hsing from the Sheng-hsin Chapter in Japan brought with him a plan to disseminate the True Buddha Dharma in Japan.

Lian-jung from Sao Paulo, Brazil had plans to translate the books of Living Buddha Lian-sheng into Portuguese.

The Edmonton and Vancouver Chapters in Canada, as well as the Hsin-fa Chapter in Hong Kong, will be responsible for the translation of the Guru's books into English.

36. Questions and Answers on the Black Sect (The Bon Religion)

An expert researching the field of world religions found my book *Hei Jiao Hei Fa* (*The Black Sect and Black Magic*) quite interesting and decided to pay me a special visit. During our meeting, he raised many questions on the Black (Bon) Sect. I have sorted out our conversations and present them below in a question and answer format. I believe the publishing of this article will provide a satisfactory and overall understanding to the origin and development of the Tibetan Black Sect.

Question: When and where did the Bon Religion originate?

Answer: The Bon Religion was originally an animist-shamanist religion that developed in the Tibetan highlands. According to the *Yung-drung Bon Chiao Shih* (A History of the Yung-drung Bon Religion), the Bon Religion had been in existence as early as 400 B.C.. Originating in Zhang-zhung, it was later introduced into the Yar-klung Valley. The fact that the original Bon Religion was an animist-shamanist religion is undisputed.

Question: What is an animist-shamanist religion?

Answer: An animist-shamanist religion arises when people harbor fears, suspiciousness, and hope towards objects found in nature and start to worship them. The most important tenet in the Bon Religion was that everything had a spirit; they therefore worshipped the heaven, the earth, the sun, the moon, mountains, rivers, thunder, lightning, hail, fog, and even birds and animals.

Question: Are there other religions similar to the Bon Religion?

Answer: From my understanding, in northeastern China, Mongolia, and even the highland areas in Taiwan, other tribes practiced similar shamanism and sorcery. In fact, animist-shamanist religious practices have been found all over the earth, preceding the development of theology-based religions. Animist-shamanist religions form the earliest known religious practices.

Question: What did the Bon believers worship?

Answer: According to chronicles of Tibet, Bon believers revered ghosts and sorcery and regarded the ibex, a high mountain goat, as god. They deified and worshipped yaks, goats, and sheep because these animals played intimate roles in their daily lives. The horns of yaks and goats were used in sacrificial rituals and especially treasured as precious vessels.

Question: How was the world divided according to the Bon Religion?

Answer: Followers of the Bon Religion believed the world was divided into three spheres: the upper Heaven sphere, the middle Earth sphere, and the lower Underworld sphere, the latter of which was inhabited by demons. In Heaven there lived six gods who were brothers. The greatest god "Samba"* was regarded as the creator of the universe. Bon followers also worshipped Dragon gods (kLu) who ruled over the human world. There were also mountain, water, and earth spirits

146

collectively known by the name gNyan. The god of the powerful Thang-lha mountain chain was also known as "the Great gNyan."

Question: Why was the Black Sect called the Bon Sect?

Answer: Most religions have spokespersons. Otherwise known as priests, they serve as go-betweens among gods, humans, and demons. The priests of the Black Sect were called "Bon-pos" in the Tibetan language. The Black Sect was therefore also called the Bon-po Religion, or Bon for short. The priests of the Black Sect were divided into three ranks: heavenly Bon-pos, earthly Bon-pos, and high Bon-pos.

Question: In your book, *Hei Jiao Hei Fa*, you pointed out that the Black Sect worshipped yaks. Do you have proof of this?

Answer: Around the fourth century B.C., the Black Sect had already formed its own religious system. At the time, a tribal chief gNya-khri bTsan-po from the Yar-klung district became the first king of central Tibet. He had come from a tribe known as the Six Yak-bulls who worshipped yaks as gods. It was with the support of the Bon Religion that gNya-khri bTsan-po became king. This was why I mentioned the Black Sect worshipped the yak gods.

Question: How did the Bon priests make a living?

Answer: The Black or Bon Religion in Tibet has had twenty-seven generations. In the past, the Bon priests were very powerful. They engaged in prayers and rituals to invoke blessings from heaven, to effect healing, to conduct divinations, to aid in business deals, and also to settle disputes. They also engaged in practices aimed to bring misfortune or punishment in the form of illnesses and deadly hail storms, and they called upon wicked ghosts to commit assaults and evil deeds on others. At that time, the Bon-pos had a great influence in many aspects of life, including fertility, marriage, healing, funerals, relocation, travel, agriculture, hunting, grazing, and the government. The Bon Religion was actually in control of the whole of Tibet, as everything had to be approved by the Bon-pos.

Question: Were there different factions in the Black or Bon Religion?

Answer: Yes, there were more or less three factions. The first, Du-Bon*, was founded by Ni-sin*. This faction was popular in Eastern Tibet and reached its height during the reign of king Da-hri Tsan-po*. The second faction, Cha-Bon*, was founded by the three Bon priests from Kashmir. This group flourished during the reign of sPu-lde Gung-rgyal up until the establishment of the Tibetan Dynasty. The third faction, Chueh-Bon*, was founded by Ching-chun Pan-chih-ta* and flourished around the time Buddhist Tantrayana was introduced into Tibet.

Question: What were the responses of the Bon Religion when Buddhist Tantrayana was first brought into Tibet?

Answer: When Tantrayana Buddhism was introduced into Tibet, it entered a long period of fighting with the Bon Religion—this is the famous struggle between Buddhism and Bon. According to the annals of the Tibetan history of religions, as soon as Buddhism entered Tibet, it immediately met with resentment and resistance from the traditional Bon Religion. This is understandable. The intense and protracted rivalry between Tantrayana Buddhism and the Bon Religion lasted over two hundred years.

Question: Did Tantrayana Buddhism finally win?

Answer: Yes. That is the main reason why I advocate that we should not blur the distinction between Tantrayana Buddhism and the Tibetan Bon Religion.

Question: Does the Bon Religion have its own scriptures?

Answer: The Bon Religion originally had no scriptures of

its own. When Buddhism was introduced into Tibet, it brought many sutras and much literature. This caused great shock among the Bon Religion adherents. They attempted to defeat Buddhism with comparable weapons and took section II (chapters 51 to 80) of the *Yogacara-bhumi* and changed it to the *Bon Sutra*. They also appropriated the *Great Dharani Sutra* and changed it into their own *White Dragon Sutra* and *Black Dragon Sutra*. The *Prajna Hundred Thousand Praises* was changed into the *Bon-po Kanjur*. It is pitiful and laughable that, after stealing these Buddhist texts, the Bon-pos then claimed their texts had been copied by Buddhist authors.

Question: When was Buddhism introduced into the Tibetan area?

Answer: Buddhism was first introduced around the seventh century, during the reign of the Tibetan King Srong-btsan sgam-po. Some records also claim that, during the reign of Lha-tho-tho-ri, the fifth predecessor of the above-mentioned king, Buddhism had been introduced into Tibet. Buddhism was of course brought into Tibet from India, but there was also a myth alleging that a treasure trunk containing Buddhist writings, a stupa, and Buddhist statues had fallen from Heaven.

Question: Can you briefly describe the Bon Religion's attempts to suppress Buddhism?

Answer: According to *Chronicles of the Tibetan Kings*, there were the following events:

1) During the building of the Jo-khang Cathedral, construction accomplished during the day was sabotaged by Bon followers at night.

2) In order to alleviate the struggles between the Buddhist and Bon groups, the royal court compromised by adding Bon symbols around the outside of the cathedral.

3) During the ministry of the powerful mGar family, Buddhist monks were expelled and Buddhist sutras were

suppressed. Both large and small cathedrals were shut down, and an image of Shakyamuni Buddha brought by Princess Wen-ch'eng was buried underground.

4) Tibetan ministers who were Bon followers interpreted an epidemic of smallpox as a sign of the wrath of ancient gods and attributed the outbreak to the Buddhist monks. They laid the blame on Princess Chin-cheng and instigated riots against the Tang Dynasty and Buddhism.

5) During the period when Na-lang-shi* assisted the king, Buddhist statutes were buried underground, the Jo-khang became an execution ground, and a decree was issued suppressing Buddhism throughout the country.

6) Anti-Buddhist Bon ministers claimed Shantarakshita, the Indian Buddhist teacher, had induced the wrath of the Bon-po gods and brought famine to Tibet. They succeeded in securing a temporary expulsion of Shantarakshita to Nepal.

7) Padmasambhava fought and subjugated the Bon priests finally allowing Buddhism to thrive in Tibet.

This complicated struggle between Bon and Buddhism lasted for more than two hundred years. During the reign of King gLang-dar-ma, there was another upsurge to revive Bon and eliminate Buddhism and the Dharma. Apart from the destruction of temples and monasteries and the burning of Buddhist books, upper level monks were murdered, middle level monks were expelled, and ordinary monks were forced to return to secular life. During this period of oppression of the Dharma in Tibet, all overt Buddhist activities were suppressed.

It is a historical fact that Buddhism and the Bon Religion were two irreconcilable rivals, and this has been recorded throughout the whole of Tibetan history. Tantrayana Buddhism and the Bon Religion are two distinct religions and should not be confused as one.

Question: Can you talk about the struggle between

Padmasambhava and the Bon priests?

Answer: Shantarakshita suggested that the Tibetan King invite Padmasambhava to Tibet to subjugate the Bon sorcerers. Padmasambhava was the great Tantrayana master in Udyana, the modern city of Kashmir. On his journey, Padmasambhava started conquering the Bon shamans. The details are recorded in the biography of Padmasambhava. Of course, Padmasambhava was a true Tantrayana master, far more capable than the Bon-pos. This enabled him to finally gain the upper hand.

Padmasambhava also adopted a new strategy. After subduing the great mountain and water spirits of the Bon Religion, he turned them into the Dharma Protectors of Buddhism. Among the Bon spirits, there are the "twelve Dan-mas"* who have all become Tantrayana Dharma Protectors. The following is a description of Padmasambhava in the religious history of Tibet. "Using his transcendental and miraculous powers, Padmasambhava subjugated the maras and non-humans who vowed from then on to turn to goodness and protect the righteous Dharma."

Question: It was said that during the struggle between Buddhism and Bon, there was a great debate. What do you know about this?

Answer: At the height of their antagonism against Buddhism, the Bon followers included in their prayers the following verse, "May the Bon ruler sTonpa gShenrab trample upon the lotus throne of Shakyamuni." They aimed their insults directly at Shakyamuni Buddha. At the time, twenty-seven noblemen had requested the king abandon the Bon Religion to study Buddhism. King Khri-srong lde-btsan therefore decided to organize a debate between Bon and Buddhism. The Bon doctrines were very shallow and no match for Buddhism's profound philosophy and doctrines. The Bon-pos naturally lost the debate. As a result, the royal court announced that Bon was to become an illegal religion, and neither members of the military nor civilians were to practice it. Finally, the Bon followers had to go underground.

Question: Can you describe the development of exoteric and esoteric Buddhism in Tibet?

Answer: Many people are aware that Buddhism was first introduced into Tibet primarily in the Sutrayana form. During the later period of introduction, people engaged in both exoteric and esoteric practices. When Tantrayana became popular in India, many famous Tantric teachers came to Tibet through Kashmir. As esoteric Tantrayana methods can greatly accelerate the process of Enlightenment, these methods became very popular in Tibet, a society that had long undergone upheavals and turbulence.

Question: Is Bon a sect of Tantrayana Buddhism?

Answer: Bon was originally an animist-shamanist religion in the Tibetan highlands and, from the beginning, was never Tantrayana. Buddhism and Bon have engaged in struggles for hundreds of years. Bon is fundamentally distinct from Buddhism and not a part of Tantrayana. As for Bon followers who became Buddhists, we can only regard them as converts from the Bon Religion to Buddhism. Tantrayana is Tantrayana, Bon is Bon, and the two should not be confused. Passing Bon off as Tantrayana is deceiving and confounding and serves no purpose at all!

*Note: All names denoted by * are transliterations of Chinese terms.*

37. Essential Oral Teachings
from Living Buddha Lian-sheng, Founder
of the True Buddha School

---

1. Zen, Tantrayana, and Stability

To reach Enlightenment, a Zen practitioner works specifically with the "nature of the mind" to explore and experience its "empty nature."

In contrast, a Tantrayana practitioner begins first with the "body." The employment of mudras, mantras, and visualization, the engendering of light in one's heart, inner fire and light drops, the opening of three channels and seven chakras, and the merging of oneself with the Light of the Universe are practices that work with the internal body. These are practices that will lead one to Enlightenment.

The Zen path to Enlightenment is comparatively more elusive. The path to Enlightenment in Tantrayana is more concrete. This is the major difference between the two.

But no matter to which world religion or particular sect within a certain religion one belongs, whether it be Zen, Tantrayana, or the Pure Land tradition within the Buddhist faith, the absolute requisite to accomplishing anything is the cultivation of stability. Without stability, there will be no Enlightenment. Without stability, a Tantric practitioner will not succeed in any of the Tantric practices. There will be no "accomplishment of inner fire" or "engendering of light in the heart." And one will definitely not be able to "merge and become one with the Light of the Universe."

Therefore, to realize Enlightenment, one must enter the state of "stability" or stillness. In the state of stability, all thoughts are gathered into "One." From "One," one enters into "Zero." One has to enter the state of "Zero" to have Emptiness. Once the seeker is grounded in Emptiness, the Light of the Universe will immediately flow into one, and one's heart will open to reveal the inherent light. Immediately the two lights will merge, and with this Merging and Immersion, there will be Enlightenment.

Stability is therefore very important.

However, if one craves fame, profit, power, the title of a master, and the ability to perform miracles, one will have many emotional afflictions. These afflictions will cause the heart to close. If the mind (heart) cannot release these emotional afflictions, how can one enter into stability?

During ordinary times, one has to develop an open mind and an open heart to be able to let go of attachments. Only when emotional afflictions are eliminated will one be able to enter into stability.

Therefore, our view of life, our methods of coping with daily stresses, and the coming and going of events have important bearings on our lives!

2. What is a "Blessing"?

Is a "Blessing" merely the guru placing his hand on your head and patting you? What is the meaning of a Blessing? One can find an analogy for a Blessing in the batting of a baseball.

A swing of the bat can send a ball flying through the air. If, at that precise moment, a gust of wind appears, carrying the ball farther than it would have otherwise traveled, this gust of wind is a "Blessing"! If you had not hit the ball and sent it flying through the air, this gust of wind would not serve you any purpose.

3. The Key to Mantra Chanting

When chanting mantras, you should use your mind power to transmit and instill the sound and its frequency into your heart chakra.

While you are chanting a mantra 108 times, do the following visualization:

Visualize a white lotus inside your heart gradually opening to full bloom. Upon the lotus sits the seed syllable Hum *. The Hum syllable emits a beam of strong white light that travels along your central channel from the heart chakra, through the throat chakra, to the crown chakra. (Chant the Guru's Heart Mantra 108 times.)

4. The Key to Entering Samadhi

During Samadhi, one quiets the mind to enter into stability. (Use visualization to guide the mind to enter the Great Luminosity of Samadhi.) Do the following visualization:

Visualize a white lotus in full bloom inside the heart chakra. The seed syllable Hum * emits a white light which travels from the heart chakra all the way up to the crown chakra. (Pause briefly in this visualization.)

Visualize a small white lotus seat appearing above your crown. Living Buddha Lian-sheng (wearing the Five Buddha Crown with the two side strips and a yellow Dharma robe

155

topped by a red cassock) holds the Padmakumara Mudra and sits on this white lotus seat resting directly on the crown opening. (Pause briefly.)

Living Buddha Lian-sheng transforms into a swirl of white light above your head. This white light becomes stronger and stronger, like the sun directly on top of one's head. (Pause briefly.)

Visualize this swirl of white light entering your crown opening, descending down the central channel, passing through the throat, until it reaches the heart chakra. (Pause briefly.)

Living Buddha Lian-sheng now sits on the white lotus seat in the heart chakra emitting brilliant white light—this is like having the sun inside your heart. (Pause slightly longer to help train the heart chakra to emit light.)

The Dharma Body of Living Buddha Lian-sheng in the heart gradually enlarges until It reaches the same size as one's body and merges with it. (Pause briefly.)

There is now no difference between Living Buddha and yourself. You are Living Buddha Lian-sheng, wearing the Five Buddhas Crown with the two side strips, wearing a string of mantra beads, donning a yellow Dharma robe topped by a red cassock, holding the Padmakumara Mudra and sitting on a large lotus seat. Residing in the spiritual realm, you have the same perfect countenance and full majesty as that of a Buddha. All Buddhas, Bodhisattvas, and Dharma Protectors are sitting around you in circles. (Pause briefly.) (Merging of Self and Living Buddha Lian-sheng)

The heart chakra Hum * in you, Living Buddha Lian-sheng, now emits strong white lights, radiating out to the ten directions of the Universe. (Pause briefly.)

All Buddhas and Bodhisattvas emit great white lights, illuminating the ten directions of the Universe. The whole Universe is filled with a great luminosity. (Pause briefly.)

Immerse yourself into this great luminosity. Becoming self-less, with neither thought nor thinking, immerse and abide in the Great Luminosity of the Ocean of Vairocana of Samadhi....

the Sanskrit seed syllable "Hum":

38. A Trip to Redmond

By Master Lian-han

M any fellow students who have traveled on pilgrimages to the Lei Tsang Temple (Ling Shen Ching Tze) in Redmond, Washington are familiar with the beautiful sights there. The majestic and lofty temple, towering pine trees, emerald Lake Sammamish, red tiles and white walls of the True Buddha Tantric Quarter, and the unusually fresh air and serene environment have all left indelible impressions on the minds of visitors.

I was very blessed and fortunate to have the opportunity to fly to Seattle on June 23rd, 1986 to pay homage to the True Buddha Tantric Quarter and Lei Tsang Temple (Ling Shen Ching Tze) and join in the birthday celebration for His Holiness Living Buddha Lian-sheng, the founder of our school.

During my five weeks stay at the temple, I had the opportunity to get close to the Living Buddha and, in his presence, receive a continuous showering of the Buddha Light. In order to share this Dharma Taste with everyone, I have written this article "A Trip to Redmond."

Birthday Celebration

On June 23rd, the eighteenth day of the fifth lunar month, I awoke early at the break of dawn to go to the Ling Shen Ching Tze Temple. At that hour, it was still very quiet. I looked admiringly at everything around me and began to videotape the scenery.

This day was the birthday of His Holiness Living Buddha Lian-sheng. The sun was rising from the horizon, and its golden rays shone on the roof tiles of the Ling Shen Ching Tze. With its reddish yellow roof turning suddenly glittering gold, the temple, a sacred place for hundreds of thousands of fellow disciples around the world, looked even more majestic than usual. Bathed in the golden sunlight, my heart filled with a reverent joy, and I looked carefully at every tree and bush around me, taking in my surroundings. Finally I fixed my gaze on the True Buddha Tantric Quarter. Our Holy Guru, Living Buddha Lian-sheng, a supremely enlightened adept, revered by hundreds of thousands of students, was living inside this building.... Just then, out of nowhere, a crow that could chant mantras suddenly cried out the long sound "Ah!" It punctured the quiet in the air and aroused me from my thoughts.

In the afternoon, students coming for the celebration began arriving at the temple. Filled with great sincerity and reverence, they had come from around the world to take part in this joyful occasion. The abbot of Ling Shen Ching Tze, Master Lian-huo (John Chen) and his two brothers and their families had already prepared a sumptuous buffet and a huge birthday cake. Everything was ready for the arrival of the Grand Master, His Holiness Living Buddha Lian-sheng.

Around 5:00 p.m., His Holiness, accompanied by shi-mu [the master's wife], walked inside the temple. Everyone crowded around them and, after escorting them to their seats, the students began to prostrate three times to honor them. But, after the first prostration, His Holiness and shi-mu stood up, turned around to face the shrine, and prostrated together with us all to the Buddhas and Bodhisattvas.

His Holiness was wearing an apricot colored monk's robe and a pair of gray monk's shoes. His round face was as compassionate as a Buddha's, and he was completely unassuming and modest, without the airs one might assume of a founder of a school or a Living Buddha. He frequently joined us in laughter.

Written on the huge birthday cake were the words: "Congratulations and Happy Birthday, Living Buddha Lian-sheng." After the lighting of the candle on the cake, everyone applauded and sang Happy Birthday. The Grand Master smiled at everyone and, when the singing was over, he bent over to blow out the candle. Everyone cheered and the entire congregation filled with jubilation. As the group of more than two hundred people focused their gaze on the Grand Master, he slowly cut a straight line across the cake and spoke in Taiwanese, "A straight road up the path!" He said the Dharma phrase in such a humorous tone that everyone broke out in laughter.

Amidst the laughter, I thought to myself, "How many people actually understand the sincerity and earnest wishes behind His Holiness' words?"

Outside the temple, people were eating and drinking. At this time, the Grand Master picked up the first slice of cake and placed it on the plate I was holding with both of my hands...

After satisfying the students' requests to have pictures taken with him, His Holiness gave a Dharma teaching with everyone sitting around him.

A Side Trip to Vancouver

At 1:00 p.m., on June 27th, 1986, His Holiness and his family, Master Lian-shi and his family, and others (altogether eleven people) got into a van and drove from the Ling Shen Ching Tze to Vancouver, Canada. His Holiness had been invited to teach for two days at the Pootee Tang, the Vancouver chapter of the True Buddha School. We also planned to visit the World Expo that was being held in Vancouver during that time.

Early summer on the west coast of North America was much like late autumn in Hong Kong. The air was cool, bright, and crystal clear. The sky was an infinite stretch of blue with only a few wisps of cloud floating by—we had picked the perfect day to begin our outing. Along the way, we passed picturesque scenery and everyone was in high spirits. His Holiness was cheerful and chatted humorously with us.

When we reached the Canadian border, the Dharma brothers from Vancouver had already been waiting there for some time. After giving His Holiness a warm welcome, our two parties started driving towards Vancouver.

When we arrived at our destination, it was almost five o'clock. Instead of going to the hotel for a rest or a restaurant for dinner, His Holiness wanted to visit the venue where the Dharma Ceremony would be held. Matters relating to the dissemination of the Buddhadharma were foremost in his mind.

At the venue, the staff of Pootee Tang was working frantically to set up the shrine. Since the Dharma Ceremony to be held the next day was an important event, there was a sense of seriousness and urgency in the air. When His Holiness arrived, the workers all dropped what they were doing and ran hurriedly over to pay homage to him.

Then, about seven or eight of the workers started excitedly

reporting to His Holiness that they had seen with their own eyes a rainbow-colored dragon in the sky earlier during the day. Everyone was trying to talk at the same time and there was intense excitement on every face. When His Holiness heard the news, he just smiled and did not say anything. Since I was an impatient person, I interrupted and questioned them, "What kind of rainbow-colored dragon? Under what circumstances did you see it?"

"I was the first one to see it while we were loading the wood works into the truck," said one Dharma brother.

"We were in a wide open area and could see the sky for miles around. The dragon looked like cloud or mist, only it wasn't, and it was semi-transparent and rainbow colored," said another Dharma brother.

"When we all saw it, the rainbow-colored dragon was flying slowly in the sky!"

"What time was it when you saw it?" I asked.

"It was earlier this afternoon, around one o'clock!"

"Which direction was the colored dragon coming from? To where was it flying?" I asked.

"It was in the sky to the south, and it was flying with its head towards the northwest."

"Was it very clear? Why didn't you take a picture of the colored dragon?"

"We all saw it very clearly. We were in the middle of moving the woods and nobody had a camera. When we wanted to go and get one, the rainbow-colored dragon disappeared!"

"No pictures, what a pity!" I scratched my head in frustration. His Holiness looked at me smiling. Suddenly the significance of the direction and time the dragon was seen dawned on me. The dragon was coming from the south—wasn't Redmond to the south of Vancouver? Flying towards the northwest—wasn't that the direction one had to travel to reach

Vancouver from Redmond? Around one o'clock—wasn't that the time His Holiness left the Ling Shen Ching Tze to come up to Vancouver?

Oh! Now I understood! The manifestation of the rainbow colored dragon was the auspicious sign accompanying the outing of a great sage! I was moved beyond words and turned my eyes towards His Holiness. He was smiling at me. In that one moment, his eyes spoke to me and I understood tacitly and felt a vibrant energy running through my body.

The Dharma Ceremony in Vancouver

At 1:00 p.m., on June 28th, the Dharma Ceremony officially began. His Holiness and the other masters walked into the venue and took seats on the stage. There was a great turnout in the audience and everyone sat quietly and reverently to hear His Holiness teach.

His Holiness first gave an introduction to the True Buddha School and its guiding principles of, "Revering the Guru, Cherishing the Dharma, and Engaging in Actual Practice." Then His Holiness encouraged everyone to practice diligently in order to reach realization and Buddhahood.

During the ceremony, His Holiness asked the Dharma brothers who had seen the rainbow-colored dragon the day before to raise their hands. Right away, seven people raised their hands.

After His Holiness gave everyone a blessing, the ceremony concluded auspiciously.

Before the ceremony the next day, His Holiness stood with everyone outside the entrance of the venue for pictures. When the pictures were developed later, one of them showed a great patch of white light over the area where His Holiness and everyone had been standing under a red banner—but everyone had disappeared. This photograph became one of several dozens of light photographs demonstrating the miraculous powers of His Holiness. His Holiness later included this picture in his new book, *Yuen Ting Ti Shen Su (Reflections on Renouncing the Home Life.)*

At the second day's ceremony, in order to arouse people's interest and facilitate the dissemination of the Dharma, His Holiness transmitted a simple Wealth God Practice to everyone.

When His Holiness was giving everyone the empowerment for the practice, I saw shi-mu and their children (Fo-ching and Fo-chi) waiting at the end of the line. When they came up, they prostrated reverently to His Holiness and, after receiving the empowerment, they respectfully placed their prepared offerings into the offering box. This made me feel extremely moved and ashamed, because the group of masters on stage (including me) had not prepared any offerings to give to His Holiness for the empowerment. Shi-mu's genuine guru devotion, despite being the guru's wife for all these years, had put us to shame.

After the successful completion of the two days' Dharma Ceremonies, we went with His Holiness on June 30th to visit the World Expo. The theme of the Expo was "transportation" and there were throngs of visitors everywhere. His Holiness was totally free and natural in our company. He talked and laughed cheerfully with us as we walked around, visiting a total of nine exhibition pavilions that day.

That evening, I said good-bye to His Holiness and shi-mu because I was going to Calgary by myself the next morning. My four days stay at Vancouver had created extra work for the Dharma brothers at Pootee Tang. Apart from organizing the business related issues for the Dharma Ceremonies, they also took the time to arrange our room, board, and transportation. I was very grateful for the sincere warmth they extended to me.

Mountains of Letters to His Holiness

On July 5th, when I arrived back in Redmond from Calgary, His Holiness had already returned from his trip three days ago. After being so busy for more than ten days, I thought life would resume again at a normal pace.

But His Holiness and shi-mu, Master Lian-hsiang, were even busier than before. Many of the more than one hundred thousand students from around the world had sent birthday cards. Since His Holiness had not been able to reply to any mail while he was away during his six-day trip to Vancouver, the letters were piling up fast. So His Holiness asked me to help with the replies to the letters.

At the True Buddha Tantric Quarter, His Holiness showed me into his bedroom. As soon as I walked in, I saw three huge baskets filled with letters. In addition, there was another pile on top of the desk and yet another next to the baskets. I could not guess how many letters there were, but my eyes almost popped out when I saw them. The number of letters had far exceeded my expectations.

Yet His Holiness only smiled. He took me to shi-mu's room and, inside, there were two desks, both piled high with letters! Oh Heavens! It was totally beyond my imagination!

"Help me, Buddhas and Bodhisattvas, I am soon going to be buried alive by these letters!" His Holiness couldn't help laughing after uttering these words.

Actually His Holiness has reached the state where sorrow is no-sorrow and happiness is no-happiness—a state of total imperturbability. Although there was great pressure from the amount of incoming mail, he was still free, relaxed, and cheerful!

After removing his chair from his room and placing it beside one of the desks in shi-mu's room, His Holiness asked me to sit across from him. Shi-mu then sat down to work at the other desk. Thus, the three of us started the "Mail Reply Company" and plunged ourselves into the high pressure and demanding job.

Each Reply Accompanied by Blessings

Actually, other than His Holiness, I could think of no one else in the world who would have been able to reply to this mountain of incoming letters. Anyone with even a slight knowledge of the kinds of requests made in these letters would know the truth of my statement.

As I had found out, although a portion of these letters asked about problems related to the study and practice of Dharma, most requested bestowals of blessing and fortune. Many sought to take refuge but, at the same time, their letters included a dozen other questions. Many of these refuge seekers suffered problems in finances, love, and health, and some asked for help on behalf of family members who were depressed or suffered from other mental disorders. They all requested the Living Buddha's blessings. In addition, many letters asked the Living Buddha to give them life readings. Some letters requested blessings and psychic readings, while others requested refuge taking and psychic readings. There were all kinds of requests in these letters.

In the pile of letters I was reading, I came across many accounts of incredibly strange happenings, as well as descriptions of many unusual and recalcitrant illnesses that were resistant to medical treatment. Revealed in these letters were also some very strange opinions and ideas.

One type of letter left me wondering whether I should laugh

or cry—the senders had taken the Living Buddha to be a fortune-teller. They asked the Living Buddha to foretell "when the daughter-in-law would give birth to a grandson," "when they would make big money," "when they would get married," "what the profession of the future husband would be," "when business would improve," "when a cheating husband would repent and come back home," etc..

Many questions were quite trivial, such as "How many sticks of incense should I burn?" "What does the Seven Star Footstep mean? Does it refer to seven moles on the human skin?" "Why does one's mood fluctuate?" "Is the orientation of my house, which faces west, a good one?" I also came across this strange question, "Should I kill my father? He is a bad person and scolds my mother and family everyday. I want to get rid of him for the sake of everyone's welfare."

Reading the pile of letters brought me face to face with the myriad kinds of people in the world. It was also awe inspiring to watch His Holiness deal with the letters and the difficult problems asked. Never did he show any annoyance at the triviality or silliness of the questions. Several letters had been written in tiny, sloppy handwriting that exceeded a dozen pages, yet did not say much at all. After reading three or four pages, one still wondered what the point of the letter was. Yet, no matter how trifling or absurd some letters seemed, Grand Master read them and replied just the same. His patience and tolerance were amazing.

The way Grand Master read these letters astonished me even more. A fast reader could typically read five to ten lines at a glance. Yet the rate at which Grand Master read the letters far exceeded that. He only needed to hold the letter in his hand and concentrate for a moment, and he would know its entire contents. Sometimes, by merely flipping through a letter that had more than ten pages, he would know the exact questions being asked. Though such abilities appear totally miraculous to our eyes, they are very ordinary for the Grand Master.

In helping with the replies, I was often baffled by the difficulty of the problems raised and would ask the Grand Master for guidance. He would take a quick glance at the letter and immediately offer the solution. No matter how strange or complicated the problem, the Grand Master never had to pause to think about it. He would always give me an answer that directly addressed and solved the problem. This astonished me greatly. Had I not witnessed it myself, I would have considered such a feat only possible in stories from Tales from the Arabian Nights.

The way His Holiness replied to the letters was even more inconceivable. He wrote so fast his pen seemed to fly over the paper. Without pausing to think, he addressed all questions. If a reply needed divination, he would do a divination right on the spot. If a letter asked for a blessing, he would immediately script a talisman to send with the reply. It was such a speedy and smooth operation that, in a twinkling, a reply was finished.

After placing a lotus logo or picture of a Buddha or Bodhisattva inside each letter, the Grand Master would bless the letter on the spot by chanting a Buddha epithet and blowing a breath of vital chi into the envelope before it was finally sealed. While carrying the big bundle of letters on his way to the mailbox, the Grand Master also chanted Buddha epithets continuously. Thus, suffused in every reply was the vital chi and spiritual light from His Holiness. These blessings were so precious that their receivers were indeed the luckiest of people!

Letters from people seeking refuge constituted the largest group and came from people from all walks of life. Buddhist monks and nuns, college professors, scholars with doctorate degrees, housewives, students, soldiers, and even people with crippling disabilities wrote in to take refuge. His Holiness displayed great compassion and equanimity while drawing sentient beings to come and take refuge in him. Quite a few letters from people seeking refuge came from entire families and large groups of people. The arduous task of filling out the refuge certificates fell on the shoulders of shi-mu, who was also responsible for writing the reply envelopes. Under the pen of shi-mu, piles of refuge certificates and countless numbers of True Buddha students were born every day. In this way, shi-mu has proved herself to be the great mother of one hundred twenty thousand students all around the world.

During this period, I noticed that many people writing to ask for refuge, divination, or blessing had not enclosed any offerings with their letters. Even those asking the Grand Master to perform Tantric rituals on their behalf did not enclose offerings with their requests. In those cases, His Holiness not only had to pay for the return postage, the printing cost for the certificates, but also the flowers and fruits purchased as offerings for the rituals. Despite this, His Holiness and shi-mu responded to these requests equally, without discrimination. They would rather live frugally, so as to save money to spend on the students. Such is the heart of His Holiness, a great and compassionate true sage, who has engendered a great vow to deliver and draw all beings equally to him!

In these sessions, when His Holiness came upon letters that were very sad, his face could not help but show great compassion. He would shake his head and sigh, "What misery!" Upon reading letters that were full of praise or gratitude, however, there would only be a faint, indifferent smile upon his face. If a letter was from a deceiving student, harboring dark intentions, he would shake his head and sigh, "How pitiful!" Yet he would still grant the wish with the hope that one day, the student would gain insight into and turn away from his evil ways.

His Holiness once made a remark that I will never forget, "As long as someone turns a single thought towards the Buddha, I will regard him or her as the Buddha!" Such is the state of mind of our Grand Master, the Holy Living Buddha!

Here I would like to appeal to fellow students from around the world to take note of the following three points when writing to the Living Buddha:

1) Do not treat the Living Buddha as a fortune-teller and bother him with trivial or mundane questions, as this wastes his precious time.

2) Do not ask the Living Buddha for instructions on insignificant matters. To consult with the Master on urgent matters, write briefly and concisely.

3) When requesting refuge or other services, please remember to include an offering. We students should make regular offerings to our lineage root guru and also adhere to the traditional practice of never making a request without an offering. Especially within the Tantric tradition, making offerings to one's root guru is considered one's first obligation. Although the Living Buddha does not mind whether or not one makes an offering to him (he always allows people to pay whatever they like without stipulating a fixed price), it is impolite for a student to make an empty-handed request. It is in fact a Tantric taboo for a student to make a request without an offering. There are many reasons why such a rule exists.

A Regimented Life and Inexhaustible Energy

His Holiness attends to a myriad of affairs every day and is extremely busy, but he lives a very disciplined and regimented life, as he did when he was in military service.

Every morning at 6:30 a.m., His Holiness rises and, after

practicing a sadhana, he writes. After eating breakfast at 8:30 a.m., he continues to write until 11:30 a.m. when he goes outside to exercise, running slowly around the temple once. After lunch at 12:00 noon, he spends the next thirty minutes or so opening mail. At 1:00 p.m. sharp, he begins replying to letters which he continues until 4:00 p.m.. He receives his visitors daily between 4:00 p.m. and 6:30 p.m.. Dinner is usually at 7:00 p.m. but sometimes delayed until 8:00 p.m. if visitors show up at the last moment or ask too many questions. Then after a bath and another session of sadhana, His Holiness takes a stroll outdoors to give some thought to his writings for the next day. After dark (Seattle's summers become dark around 9:30 p.m.), he opens more letters and reads some books. Sometimes he will play the piano or watch television to improve his English. Before retiring at midnight, he often sips a small glass of mild wine. This timetable is followed strictly except for evenings when visitors may cause delays in this schedule.

What amazes me most is that, despite this very busy schedule, His Holiness is always energetic. He has never taken afternoon naps or dozed off. I have asked shi-mu about this, and she said, "It has been like this for the last nine years. It is lucky that he has so much energy; otherwise, how would he deal with so many things?" I was reminded of the time I had visited with the Living Buddha in 1983 when he was already this full of energy, never showing fatigue.

Several times I have followed His Holiness during his daily jog around the temple. On sunny days, at 11:30 a.m. sharp, he puts down his pen, does some warm up exercises in the living room, and opens the front door to go outside. After running from his house to the front of the temple, he jogs up the temple steps and turns to the right to circle the outside of the temple. Every time, upon reaching the left side of the temple, he pauses momentarily and joins palms to acknowledge the Dragon Spirit under the three tall pine trees. When he comes around to the front of the temple, he either stops again to join palms and pay respect to the Bodhisattvas inside the temple, or he will simply go inside to perform Great Homage. Afterwards, he joins his palms and bows before the outdoor incense burner before running down the steps to go home. It was a joy for me to run behind him. He looked so natural and unrestrained with the loose apricot monk's robe swaying gently in the wind, and his cheer and humor warmed me like a spring breeze.

The days were bright and sunny, with fresh air, and warm gentle breezes; I felt so blessed to be able to jog together with the carefree and unrestrained Living Buddha, as we ran slowly around the temple, surrounded by beautiful scenery. This period of time was a most unforgettable interlude in my life!

Receiving and Helping Visitors Daily

No matter how busy he is, His Holiness insists that some time be set aside each day for him to meet with visitors. When the clock in the living room strikes four in the afternoon, he puts down his mail and walks downstairs to the shrine room, the True Buddha Tantric Quarter, to greet his visitors. He sees them at a desk adjacent to the shrine where three chairs have been set up beside the window.

Every visitor coming to pay respects to His Holiness must first call shi-mu by telephone to schedule an appointment. This is the minimum courtesy one should show. Every day, at the hour of seeing visitors, the downstairs living room fills with people. This task is even more demanding than replying to the mail. Shi-mu also keeps a very busy schedule. After greeting the visitors and seating them, she hands them paper onto which they may write down their questions. Then she arranges for them to go in turn to see the Living Buddha. People waiting their turn do not always sit still. They fidget around and talk loudly, and shi-mu brings them tea, fruits, and snacks.

Visitors who come to see His Holiness come from all walks of life—they are of various nationalities and from various countries. Most of the problems presented are the conventional kind as people seek the Living Buddha for help and blessings. Among these people, there seem to be no lack of those who are long-winded and capable of pestering one beyond endurance.

Shi-mu is a very cultivated person with a good temper. No matter how long-winded the visitors are, she always faces them calmly, with a smile. One can only imagine the amazing patience and endurance the Living Buddha must have in order to satisfy the various requests posed by visitors in the shrine room.

Shi-mu said, "The Grand Master has always taught that sentient beings experience a great deal of suffering, and we should try to satisfy their wishes." One can see from this, the great compassion of the Living Buddha and shi-mu.

Because of His Holiness' renown, visitors are occasionally very nervous and excited when entering the shrine room to speak with the Grand Master. Their hearts race and they become tongue-tied. Sometimes, from the time they walk into the room to the time they walk out, they are flustered and in a daze.

I remember one lady who had taken a flight of more than twenty hours to meet with His Holiness for a consultation. After the meeting, she walked out of the room with a transfixed look upon her face. Later, when her companion came out after meeting with the Living Buddha, she asked the lady if she had prostrated to the shrine. The lady answered that she was not aware there was a shrine in the room. Everyone found it strange that she did not notice the large shrine covered with numerous Buddhist statues. She explained, "When it was my turn to go inside, I was so nervous that I don't even know how I managed to walk into the room. All I know is that the Living Buddha asked me to take a seat. After sitting down and handing him the paper I had written earlier, the Living Buddha then said something to me, but I don't remember what it was. Then I came out. I really did not see the shrine... My heart is still thumping now!" Upon hearing this, everyone laughed.

Shi-mu was indeed compassionate. At the next break, she personally took the lady into the shrine room again, so she had a chance to pay her respects before the shrine. The lady was extremely grateful afterwards.

Sometimes visitors without the courtesy to make appointments arrive unannounced. They show up at the front door, ring the bell, and are disappointed when they are politely turned away. The meeting schedule of His Holiness is so tightly booked that it is very difficult to accommodate add-ons. The compassionate shi-mu often tries to arrange appointments within a week for those who have traveled especially far to meet His Holiness. If His Holiness happens to be out of town, then visitors just have to wait until next time.

Shi-mu, A Great Woman

We are all familiar with the adage, "Behind a successful man, there is always a virtuous and able wife."

In his life, His Holiness has walked steadfastly and successfully on the path to reach "Buddhahood in the Present Life." He has succeeded in demonstrating to sentient beings that such a goal is possible. His footprints radiate sparkling golden lights guiding sentient beings who walk closely behind him.

Behind His Holiness, there is the great and compassionate shi-mu!

Shi-mu deserves great merits for her role in helping the Living Buddha. She has accompanied His Holiness during their many years of great hardship. Since their beginning with meager resources, they have endured tidal waves of malicious slanders and attacks from all directions. Supportively, behind the amazing steel-like will power and determination of His Holiness, are the comforting words, encouragement, and friendship of shi-mu. They have shared many touching stories.

Together, His Holiness and shi-mu have endured hardships and comforts, joys and sorrows. Shi-mu is the greatest Dharma supporter behind the Grand Master's achievement in realizing Buddhahood! During the process, shi-mu herself has endured trials and tribulations and gained a great deal of experience. She also has cultivated to a very high spiritual level and developed admirable powers of stability. She shows deep understanding in her ability to perfectly handle many different situations.

Shi-mu sets a superb example to others by sincerely "devoting herself to the guru, cherishing the Dharma, and actualizing the practice." Quietly, she has advanced on the pathway and gained profound understanding. Consequently she has received the Acharya Empowerment from His Holiness and become a master herself.

My wife and I first met shi-mu seven years ago, when we traveled to Redmond to seek teaching and pay homage to the Living Buddha. During that stay in 1983 of more than half a month at their house, shi-mu did not teach me any Dharma. Last year, my wife and I had the opportunity to hear shi-mu teaching at the Taipei Chuang Yan Chapter and the Taichung Chi Chieh Chapter and were greatly impressed with her wisdom and progress.

During my present stay at the Master's house, I have had the chance to chat with shi-mu on several occasions. Casually she imparted to me some gems of wisdom in her remarks. When I heard them, I was instantly amazed, secretly feeling both surprise and joy. I was surprised because she had made an inconceivable breakthrough in her cultivation; and I was happy because her remarks had unintentionally resolved a personal question I had had in my practice for a long time! The question I had was quite profound and complicated, and I had been waiting for a chance to seek His Holiness' advice. Unexpectedly, from my casual chat with shi-mu, I was able to resolve the mental knot in my mind. I immediately realized that she had reached an advanced level in her cultivation!

Shi-mu also has in her the virtues valued of traditional Chinese women: simplicity, perseverance, thrift, knowledge of running a household and teaching the children. On top of the busy housework, however, she also has a heavy load of Dharma work.

Her housework consists of taking care of the entire household: sweeping and cleaning, cooking, grocery shopping, laundry, sewing, driving the children to and from school, and taking care of the children's general needs.

In her daily Dharma work, she fills out piles of refuge certificates and piles of return envelopes for inquiring students (the total number of refuge students being 120,000 at the time of this writing.) Every day she prepares tea, fruit, and snacks for the people who have traveled from all corners of the world to pay homage to the Living Buddha, and she makes arrangements for them to see him in turn. She also listens patiently to the numerous long-distance phone calls that come at all hours from around the world. Nevertheless, her training and long-term exposure to these duties has enabled her to handle everything calmly and confidently.

Additionally, shi-mu has one more important job—the sacred task of attending to His Holiness, the Grand Master of 120,000 True Buddha School students around the world. This great service of hers in the aiding and deliverance of sentient beings will occupy a glorious page in the annals of the True Buddha School.

In educating their children, shi-mu also proves to be a model mother. In addition to helping Fo-ching and Fo-chi with their homework, she also teaches them life principles and morals. She is kind but also strict, patient and detail oriented.

I found myself very lucky to have the chance to go out every Sunday afternoon with the Grand Master and his family. One time, while visiting a downtown shopping center, Fo-chi went inside a toy store and did not come out for a long time. The Grand Master, shi-mu, and I sat down on a bench while Fo-ching went inside the store to look for him. As soon as Fo-chi came out, he wanted his mother to go into the store with him. Shi-mu resisted at first but, after a tug-of-war, she finally agreed to walk into the store. After taking a look however, she came out of the store again, with a grimacing Fo-chi in tow.

We left the toy store and continued our stroll. I noticed that behind us, Fo-chi kept turning his head to look at the store, while secretly wiping his tears. So I bent over to him and whispered, "What if you and I go quietly back to the toy store, and I buy it for you?" I had hoped this would bring a smile to his face, but he shook his head and said, "No!"

We were getting farther and farther away from the toy store. I was keeping company with Fo-chi behind and, seeing him crying, I tried three times to make him turn around to go back to the store. He continued to refuse. Finally, I asked him, "Don't you really want that toy?"

He nodded. Then I asked again, "Then why won't you go

back to the store? I will buy it for you, and your mom and dad won't scold you for it."

He answered curtly and resolutely, "My dad and mom will not be happy about it!"

I watched helplessly as this little eight-year-old Dharma brother took a tearful leave from the toy store. Yet I could not help but admire the proper way in which shi-mu had educated her son.

Golden Sun Rays in the Dark

Outside the Ling Shen Ching Tze and True Buddha Tantric Quarter, I was often lost in deep thought while gazing at the scenery around me. Here the deep blue sky made the few puffs of white clouds whiter than usual, and the emerald green lawns and heaven-reaching giant pines enhanced the gold of the temple roof tiles. What a beautiful and magnificent view! This is because a great and holy sage, His Holiness the Living Buddha, lives here! The spiritual light of the Living Buddha pervades heaven and earth and stretches from ocean to sky. Breathing in this fresh air, I felt carefree and joyous; all my worldly troubles had melted away! I raised my head to the sky and, with my eyes closed, reveled in this state wherein the self is almost forgotten...

I often stood alone at the left corner of the temple, looking up at the three tall pines. Not too long ago, His Holiness had been standing on this same spot, as the Dragon Spirit manifested above the giant pines, spewing golden lights on him...

Often in the early morning and late evening, I would go to the temple and sit behind the offering table in the center, meditating while facing the shrine. This spot is the center of the dragon den and the spiritual energy here is the strongest. Meditating here enables spiritual energy to speedily converge and fill the body; enabling one to swiftly enter a state of stability.

One night after 10 p.m., I again went to the temple to meditate alone. After assuming the full lotus, I quickly felt the spiritual energy rushing through my body. Amidst an extraordinarily concrete yet buoyant lightness, I entered into stability and became detached from my surroundings. Suddenly, the space in front of my eyes lit up and I saw the two window-panes of His Holiness' True Buddha Tantric Quarter filled with a dazzling light. This was very much like a reflection of sunlight off glass windows. Yet, upon second glance, I realized the light was not a reflection but sunlight radiating from inside out. Then there was a spread of golden, dazzling light obliterating the windows and even the walls. A rush of surprise and joy ran through my heart and, with the arising of thought, I emerged from samadhi.

Getting up on my feet, I ran out of the temple as fast as I could. (Actually I was limping because sitting in the lotus posture had made my legs slightly sore.) The two windows of His Holiness' True Buddha Tantric Quarter were dark and there was no light inside the room. I walked slowly over to the windows and listened. It was quiet and I did not hear any human sounds. Transfixed on the spot, I recalled the vision I had seen in my meditation two minutes ago.

What wonderfully bright and dazzling golden sunrays those were, appearing in the dark of night! What was the source of the light? What did it mean? I knew His Holiness would be the only person who could solve this riddle for me!

The Precious Supreme Transmission of Mind

During the nearly two months of my stay at the Ling Shen

Ching Tze Temple, what I enjoyed most was accompanying His Holiness on his walks.

Right before lunch after jogging around the temple, or right after dinner before dark, His Holiness loved taking walks and he liked me to accompany him. We sometimes walked around the temple or the True Buddha Tantric Quarter, or we would walk along the streets outside the temple compound. We would chat while walking, sometimes sitting down on the steps outside the temple.

I learned much about the Dharma and benefited greatly from these walks. His Holiness recounted to me many of his early experiences that now seemed like fairy tales. They often left me dumbstruck.

His Holiness also explained to me, "on-site," the feng-shui of the Ling Shen Ching Tze. His instructions were so clear and logical that I often found myself exclaiming with admiration!

His Holiness' earnest and tireless teachings have resolved the puzzles and doubts in my mind. With one casual, penetrating remark, he would lay bare the truth and then touch on it lightly to straighten out my muddled thinking. When I suddenly saw the core of my problems, I was so moved that hot tears rushed to my eyes.

During the time we took walks, His Holiness, like a kind father, continuously instilled the great wisdom drip by drip into this foolish child of his, opening up layers and layers of mental blockages. Like a tiny sunflower, I grew sturdily under the nourishment of plentiful sunlight and rain.

Two days after the night of my vision of the golden sunlight, at 11:00 a.m., His Holiness suddenly called to me, "Let's go for a walk!" I looked at my watch and saw that it was still too early for the morning jog. But accompanying His Holiness in his jogging and strolling were my favorite things, so I hurriedly put on my jacket and followed him downstairs.

As we walked downstairs, His Holiness started chatting to me in an ordinary tone, "Shakyamuni Buddha taught the Dharma for forty-nine years to show people one Truth. But, throughout those forty-nine years, he never explicitly stated the Truth...

"The *Diamond Sutra* says, 'If people claim that the Tathagata has taught the Dharma, then they are slandering the Buddha.' After teaching the Dharma for forty-nine years, he claimed that he had not taught the Dharma. What on earth did He mean by that? Do you understand?"

His Holiness' words were too profound for me—of course I did not understand. But, why did His Holiness bring up such a profound question that day? For a moment, I did not know his intent, so I just listened as we walked.

Outside, the warm sunlight showered upon us and, when we strolled leisurely to the front of the temple, His Holiness continued, "I have been writing books to transmit the Dharma. There are now sixty-five books filled with Dharma writings. Every time we have a Dharma ceremony and group cultivation, I also teach the Dharma, but...

"I still have not really transmitted the Dharma!"

His last statement caught me by surprise! His Holiness smiled at me, "The principle behind this is the same as that of Shakyamuni Buddha's final claim that he had not taught any Dharma after forty-nine years of teaching the Dharma.

"Remember this: all Dharmas of the phenomenal world are still Dharmas of the other side of the mountain! As the *Diamond Sutra* also says, 'all things of the phenomenal world are like dreams, bubbles, dews, or lightning!'"

Thus, His Holiness started the process of transmitting to me the most secret method of Shakyamuni Buddha—the supreme method of the Transmission of the Mind.

For over a month, His Holiness repeatedly and compassionately prepared me for the supreme mind practice. In order to help my slow-witted mind thoroughly understand him, he explained the profound truth in simple and accessible terms, and guided me systematically with skill and patience. These teachings usually took place during our strolls, sometimes while we walked around the temple or True Buddha Tantric Quarter, on roads outside the compound, or when we sat on the temple steps.

One day at noon, shi-mu came home and saw His Holiness and me sitting on the steps outside their home. She hurriedly went to prepare lunch and laughed, "Ai-ya! You poor teacher and disciple. You two must be starving!"

His Holiness was in the middle of giving me a teaching, and he seized the opportunity to humorously state, "We two are sitting at the front door waiting for our lunch. Have pity on us please!" We all broke into laughter.

The transmission of the supreme mind practice from His Holiness allowed me to truly understand the truth behind attaining Buddhahood in this lifetime and the secret mind seal of the Buddhas in the ten directions.

"Oh! So this is what it is!" I greatly marveled.

His Holiness never formally told me ahead of time that he was transmitting to me the supreme mind practice and, when it happened, he seemed to be chatting casually. When I realized suddenly that His Holiness was transmitting to me the rarely encountered secret mind practice of the Tathagata, I was moved beyond words! Later that night, when I returned to my sleeping quarter, I was so grateful I started crying and prostrating repeatedly in the direction of the True Buddha Tantric Quarter. That was how I spent numerous sleepless nights afterwards.

What amazed me even more and filled me with even greater admiration was the inconceivably high and unfathomable realm attained by His Holiness.

His Holiness is completely a living "Great Sun Tathagata"! It is a pity that mortal people are unable to recognize the precious manifestation of a true Buddha before their eyes, thereby missing this rare and valuable opportunity. Hindered by the three poisons and tempted by fame and profit, their spirituality is shrouded. How many understand what a high realm the Living Buddha has attained and what an open and infinite heart he has?

His Holiness is such a great sage!

Pitiful are those who do not recognize this!

Bodhisattva Vows and Future Ordination Vows

Here I would like to mention the occasions wherein I generated the Bodhisattva Vows and received permission from His Holiness for future renunciation.

On July 7th, 1986, His Holiness conducted a ritual for me to accept the Bodhisattva Precepts. Although few people attended, it was a very solemn occasion. At the True Buddha Tantric Quarter, I generated the Bodhisattva Vows for householders, and His Holiness gave me an empowerment and served as my witness. After the ceremony, His Holiness gave me a certificate for having accepted the rules of conduct of a bodhisattva.

Many years ago, in reading His Holiness' books, I learned that he would eventually become a monk. At the time, I thought to myself that when His Holiness became a monk, I would also follow suit and become a monk!

At the beginning of this year, when I heard that His Holiness had become a monk, my first thoughts were, "Oh this is too quick! I am not ready to leave my family life yet!" But my determination to eventually follow in the Grand Master's footsteps is still strong and unwavering! One night, in late July, I suddenly dreamt of His Holiness with a Buddha standing behind him. I knelt down to pay homage to them, and His Holiness smiled and proceeded to perform a tonsure for me.

When I told this dream to His Holiness, he nodded and said, "Very good. Let us have a ceremony to mark your future renunciation."

Therefore, on July 28th, 1986, after dinner, His Holiness performed a solemn and dignified ritual for me in the True Buddha Tantric Quarter. After snipping a tuft of my hair, he gave me a special empowerment for being prophesied by Shakyamuni Buddha to receive monkhood in the future. During the empowerment, a current of warm energy entered my crown. When the warm current reached my heart, I could feel it pausing there for a moment before spreading throughout my body. At that moment, I felt in my heart a sudden opening and an expanse of bright light. Dwelling in this state of lightness and peacefulness, I almost did not want to open my eyes.

I prostrated gratefully several times to His Holiness and the Buddhas and Bodhisattvas. His Holiness compassionately told me that, with the completion of this ritual, I could in the future have my hair shorn anywhere and anytime to become a monk. My future name after tonsure would be Shakya Lian-han.

Om Mani Padme Hum!

Free Subscriptions to the
Purple Lotus Journal!

The Purple Lotus Society has a free English journal
for anyone with an interest in Buddhism. Articles and
speeches by Living Buddha Lian-sheng concerning
Vajrayana, Ch'an (Zen) Buddhism, and Pure Land
Buddhism are featured in the journal.

To order books or be placed on the mailing list for the
Purple Lotus Journal, contact:

Purple Lotus Society Publishing
33615 - 9th Street
Union City, CA 94587
Tel: (510) 429-8808   Fax: (510) 429-7150

An Overview of the Buddhadharma
by Master Sheng-yen Lu

From May 3, 1993 to May 13, 1993, at the Rainbow Villa Retreat Center in Washington, Living Buddha Lian-sheng (Master Sheng-yen Lu), the founder of the True Buddha School, gave a series of talks on the subject of an overview of the Buddhadharma. In the numerical system outlined below, the Living Buddha presents not only a clear and concise understanding to a profound teaching, but also a concrete way to reach Enlightenment.

-The INITIAL step of "faith, comprehension, practice, and realization."

-The TWO doorways of "theoretical" versus "practical" approaches.

-The THREE non-outflow studies of "discipline, stability, and wisdom."

-The FOUR noble truths.

-The FIVE roots and FIVE positive agents.

-The SIX perfections.

-The SEVEN factors of Enlightenment.

-The EIGHTFOLD noble path.

-The TEN powers of Buddhas.

-The TWELVE links that constitute the chain of conditioned arising.

pgs. 248; $10.00

Dharma Talks by a Living Buddha
by Master Sheng-yen Lu

From Dragon Kings to Buddhahood, Master Sheng-yen Lu covers a gamut of esoteric subjects in his many dharma talks. Recognized as a Living Buddha by his students and many Tibetan tulkus, Master Lu brings a unique perspective to the Buddhadharma few others can give.

In this book, one will find out:

-How to do wealth practices to acquire abundance.

-Why sariras (signs of spiritual achievement) were found amid the cremated remains of some executed prisoners in Singapore.

-Why there is a red light district in the realm of heavens.

-Who Nagarjuna is and what his relationship to Shakyamuni Buddha is.

-How Shakyamuni Buddha learned to drink coffee.

-How to expand one's consciousness.

As the Living Buddha says, "One cannot be too aloof from the sentient beings!" In delivering these talks, the Living Buddha entered into a communion with his audiences and delivered the teachings in a way that could be understood by the capacities of all his listeners. By opening one's heart to these teachings, one will find the darkness of one's being suddenly flooded, illuminated by the Light of Truth.

pgs. 209; $10.00

Encounters with the World of Spirits
by Master Sheng-yen Lu

Grand Master Lu's unique spiritual odyssey began one day in 1969. While disinterestedly watching a Buddhist festival, Grand Master Lu was called out from the crowd by a trance medium and told the Buddhas wanted him to spread the Dharma. That night, Grand Master Lu was magically transported to the magnificent Buddha realm, known as the Maha Twin Lotus Ponds, where he was greeted by many Bodhisattvas. During the next several years, many remarkable and mysterious happenings transformed Grand Master Lu's life. An invisible teacher from the spirit realm came to teach Grand Master Lu many esoteric arts. An old Taoist teacher in the Taiwan mountains taught Grand Master Lu ancient Taoist techniques. Meanwhile, Grand Master Lu exorcised spirits from the spiritually possessed, assisted departed spirits, and spoke with various heavenly beings. This book will inspire anyone oriented towards the esoteric arts.

pgs. 198; $10.00

Four Essays on Karma
by Yuen Liao Fan

A perennial favorite in China since it was first published in the early 17th century, this book contains many gems of information on how to transform one's karma. The workings of the law of cause and effect come to life in the many examples outlined in the book. *Four Essays on Karma* follows the lives of various individuals who are faced with difficult circumstances and tells how they were able to avert these problems and live successful lives by understanding the concept of karma. What is more, the techniques mentioned in the book for transmuting karma are simple and easy to apply, by anyone at any time, to achieve a better life.

"The teachings and examples given in this book can be of tremendous benefit to us. They contain the wisdom of long ago and far away, offering—as though from a mountain—a much broader and higher perspective on basic human issues."
—Master Kender Taylor

pgs.64; $5.00

The Inner World of the Lake
by Master Sheng-yen Lu

In this book (written during the summer of 1985), Lake Sammamish in the State of Washington is transformed in the eyes of an enlightened Buddhist Master, Sheng-yen Lu, into the Lake of Self Nature (Buddha Nature). Through the Master's descriptions of the lake under various conditions, in different times and seasons, the reader can glimpse into the mind of an enlightened master and share his joys and insights in the cultivation of the Buddha Dharma.

pgs. 217; $10.00

The Mystical Experiences of True Buddha Disciples
by Master Sheng-yen Lu

After more than twenty years of Buddhist Tantric practice, Master Sheng-yen Lu, founder of the True Buddha School, has been able, during his meditational practices, to merge with the Universe. He understands the secret of the Universe and is truly Enlightened. He has become a great adept and has achieved the Six Transcendental Powers.

Miracles in this book include the curing of terminal and karmic illnesses, accurate spiritual predictions, warning of imminent disasters, and lottery winnings. The authentic cases recorded in this book represent some of the numerous cases of mystical experiences witnessed by Master Lu's students.

pgs. 167; $10.00

A Complete and Detailed Exposition on the True Buddha Tantric Dharma
by Master Sheng-yen Lu

The nuances and subtleties required for successful Tantric Buddhist practice were meticulously laid out by Grand Master Lu in a series of discourses at the Rainbow Villa in western Washington state in 1992. In these talks, Grand Master Lu shares the wealth of information he has obtained from his twenty spiritual masters so that practitioners may quickly attain spiritual response from their Personal Deity. Sharing with the reader the various visualizations, mantras, hand gestures, and breathing techniques for a highly successful practice, Grand Master Lu enables the practitioner to quickly progress toward Buddhahood. The reader can learn the methods for invoking deities, paying homage to the deities, guarding against negative forces, merging consciousness with one's Personal Deity, and entering into samadhi.

pgs. 230; $10.00

New Revelations from the Buddha King
By Master Sheng-yen Lu

In this book, Living Buddha Lian-sheng reveals the true identities of Padmakumara and the Living Buddha's invisible teacher, Mr. Three-Peaks-Nine-States. The Buddha King in the title refers to Amitabha.

Using the Wisdom of Discriminatory Awareness associated with Amitabha, Living Buddha Lian-sheng discloses the identities of the Helper Guides behind some of the contemporary Buddhist masters such as Lin Yun, Ven. Hsing yun, Ven. Ching Hai, and Ven. Hsuan Hua.

Do you know to where Confuscius has gone? What are the twenty-eight levels of heavens? What kinds of phenomena await one in the practice of the Personal Deity Yoga? In this, his 120th book, Master Lu answers these and many other questions, offering the readers glimpses into the mysterious workings of the universe.

pgs. 180; $10.00

The Annotated True Buddha Sutra
By Master Sheng-yen Lu

The *True Buddha Sutra* is short for The Sutra of Authentic Dharma that Removes Hindrances and Bestows Good Fortune. This sutra contains the authentic Buddhadharma and holds the key to eradicating one's disasters and receiving good fortune. This is tantamount to transforming one's fate. Additionally, this sutra can help one attain rebirth to the Maha Twin Lotus Ponds, the highest realm within Amitabha's Pure Land.

In this series of thirteen talks, Living Buddha Lian-sheng gives us a sincere and discerning explication of the *True Buddha Sutra*. This book describes the happenings in Maha Twin Lotus Ponds prior to Padmakumara's incarnation into the human world. Inside, the Living Buddha also divulges the secret to the many inscrutable Zen koans. Presented in his clear and lively style, *The Annotated True Buddha Sutra* in fact holds the most profound secret to achieving Buddhahood.

pgs. 119; $10.00